The Old Testament
and Christian Spirituality

Contents

Preface

FOR A GOOD DEAL of recent times in the Church there has been talk, and there have been writings, on the subject of spirituality—namely, that there is something within us humans which seeks to reach out to and have relations with the ground and purpose of our lives. In the context of Job's sufferings, the young man Elihu, son of Barachel the Buzite, opines that there is a spirit in a mortal that is nothing less than the breath of the Almighty, and this is what makes for human understanding (Job 32:8).

Gordon S. Wakefield, that minister of the Methodist Church, scholar, and saint—and I like to think for me a Father in God—sought through proclamation, writing, and his own life, to help us appreciate the deep reality of this spirituality, that there is indeed a spirit in a human person that brings them into a relationship with the Almighty. I can well remember once sharing in a letter and a telephone call with him about an ambition of mine one day possibly to write about what the Old Testament had to contribute to a Christian spirituality. He exhorted and encouraged me to get on with the task. I cannot say that I did that with any promptitude, for first there was retirement to wait and work for, and even then the spirituality task was left until "later," in fact until that stage in life when other, apparently more straightforward writing projects, were completed. Thus Gordon Wakefield did not live to see the completion of this little work, but I am sure he will be aware of it, regarding it with his critical yet ever-charitable judgments.

I have tried to write not just for scholars of spirituality, but in the first place for a much wider constituency, not least those of today's Christian churches. Thus, I have disciplined myself to write without either footnotes or endnotes, and I hope I have offered a useful but not over-challenging bibliography. For I have added a section on "Further Reading" on the subject matter of each chapter, but this only for those who may perhaps wish to pursue certain matters and aspects further—but that others may be content to leave on one side. My biblical quotations are from the New

Revised Standard Version (NRSV), in its American version; and following contemporary styles I use the abbreviations B.C.E. (before the Common Era) rather than B.C. (before Christ), and C.E. (Common Era) rather than A.D. (anno Domini). Further, there are indexes of Subjects and Biblical References, which I trust might be found useful.

I am most grateful to, and thankful for, those who have continued to be around me here on earth, encouraging, and ever-enquiring when the work might be completed. Three friends have been most helpful and constructive in their reading through the completed typescript and helping me with their comments, most of which have been incorporated into what is now presented. It was Dr. Adrian Curtis, as a professional Old Testament scholar and also leader of Methodist worship, who pointed out to me a number of matters I had not dealt with and that perhaps called for further attention, or indeed attention. Then there was Rev. David Hall, Spiritual Director and Leader of Whaley Hall Retreat Centre here in Whaley Bridge, who gave me so much encouragement for this project and when it was complete read through the whole work, and talked it over with me. And, of course, my wife Hazel has gone through the text with her proverbial fine-tooth comb, pointing out to me various repetitions that needed attention, and sundry other grammatical infelicities, all of which could have been expressed more serendipitously—or simply more clearly. Yet above all there has been her love and intellectual companionship without which I would not have got thus far—and never forgetting that help of hers in matters to do with computers and computing. I am now further grateful to Wipf and Stock for agreeing to publish another work of mine, to Justin Haskell, Robin Parry, Matthew Wimer, Daniel Lanning, Ian Creeger, and to all who have worked on the project. Yet I am still responsible for the final result, even with those now-proverbial Cromwellian "warts and all."

Thus I send out this little work, with the prayer that it may indeed be of some use and encouragement in the Church today, and that it might help us make continued use of the Old Testament both in our individual and also in our corporate spiritual searches, indeed in our Christian spirituality.

Michael E. W. Thompson

On the Festival of Saint Teresa of Avila, Teacher of the Faith

15th October 2018

Introduction

You shall love the LORD your God with all your heart, and with
all your soul, and with all your might. (Deut 6:5)

THE PSALMIST OF PSALM 4 is clearly a troubled person. Already in verse 1
he is calling out to the Lord about various sufferings he is facing and about
which he is engaged in earnest praying to the Lord that God will be gracious
to him, and, moreover, answer him in his situation of deep distress. Yet, as is
so often the case in this type of psalm, by the end of the composition there
is for the troubled psalmist a deep sense of peace expressed, as we read in
the closing verse:

I will both lie down and sleep in peace;
For you alone, O LORD, make me lie down in safety. (Ps 4:8)

This psalmist is surely expressing here, at the close and climax of his psalm,
a particular aspect of his strong assurance of hope, indeed confidence, that
he has been given in his life, a mysterious *something* that is available for him,
that *something* which mysteriously and wondrously is wholly adequate for
the troubled situation in which he finds himself.

Or consider another psalm, this one being a composition that expresses throughout its verses the psalmist's confidence in his God, this being
summed up in the concluding words, which read,

You show me the path of life.
In your presence there is fullness of joy;
in your right hand are pleasures for evermore. (Ps 16:11)

Such confidence and hope, granted through his personal relationship
with the Lord is perhaps expressed above all in the twenty-third psalm,
where, just taking two of its verses we find the words of supreme faith, hope
and overwhelming confidence:

1

> Even though I walk through the darkest valley,
>   I fear no evil;
> for you are with me;
>   your rod and your staff—
>   they comfort me.
>
> . . . . .
>
> Surely goodness and mercy shall follow me
>   all the days of my life,
> and I shall dwell in the house of the LORD
>   my whole life long. (Ps 23:4, 6)

This is an expression of the most profound confidence on the part of a believer in God for all sorts of conditions and eventualities in life. Further, it is about earthly life, but it is neither expressed in the language of, nor is it coming from the realm of, earthly life, but it is rather about what we in our day may call *spiritual* matters. It is not an expression of confidence that can be proven in and through earthly terms and arguments, but for the believer it is a reality they are able to feel assured about—both individually and corporately. Indeed, this is speaking about what is nothing less than a profound spiritual reality, expressed in the language of worship and adoration, of hope and confidence in God. Such spiritual confidence is given expression in that night prayer, in some parts of the Church known as Compline,

> In peace we will lie down and sleep;
>   for you alone, Lord, make us dwell in safety.

All this is to say that beyond the realities of mere earthly life—and yet somewhat paradoxically to be lived out in earthly life—are these dimensions of life that are centered on a spiritual relationship between the Lord and his people. This is what we might mean when we speak about *spirituality*; namely, while we live in the world lives of flesh and blood, we also have this spiritual aspect, this reality that has been called, *spirituality*. Thus, for example Thomas Merton (1915–68) who became a Trappist monk could speak of his relationship in remarkable and personal terms, saying that his personal destiny was "a meeting, an encounter with God that He has destined for me alone. His glory in me will be to receive from me something which he can never receive from anyone else."

Indeed, "spirituality" is a word we find being used a good deal in the Christian Church, and elsewhere, these days. Further, it has in recent decades come to occupy an increasingly significant place in the life of the Church, in theological study, and in the pursuit of the Christian faith on the parts of individuals and groups. However, unfortunately there is as yet no agreement upon just what is understood by "spirituality," various writers using the word to express different aspects, different nuances of the matter. What is clearer is what spirituality is *not*: it is neither some vague search for evidence of paranormal presence and/or powers, and nor is it quite the same as "theology." Rather, while we may say that theology is the rational account of religious faith, spirituality might be said to be the viewing and living of human life in terms of a conscious relationship with God, and within communities of God's people. Thus while theology may be said to be something of an intellectual pursuit of religious faith, the formulation of what religious people believe, spirituality is both about that *and also* the *practicing* of those beliefs, the prayerful attempt at a devout living out of them. Alister McGrath says that

> Spirituality is the outworking in real life of a person's religious faith—what a person *does* with what they believe. It is not just about ideas, although the basic ideas of the Christian faith are important to Christian spirituality. It is about the way in which the Christian life is conceived and lived out.

I would wish to say, rather, that spirituality is both of these—it is about both the *believing* and also the *practicing of* what we believe. Colin Alves some years ago wrote about spirituality being "concern with the transcendental" while in the same work Mollie Batten said that spirituality is "a comprehensive concept involving faith, an activity and life, all in a relation which is some kind of wholeness." Rowan Williams in a recent work speaks about the difficulties we have with this very word "spirituality," saying,

> It is a helpful shorthand to talk about spirituality and spiritual life, but we ought to be aware of just what an odd turn of phrase it is. Spirituality is really quite a modern word. If you had asked anybody in the fifteenth century, "Tell me about your spirituality," they would not have had a clue what you were talking about. "Spirituality" for the Christian is shorthand for "life in the Spirit," for staying alive in Christ.

That is, we might say that at one level spirituality is about knowing God, not just knowing *about* God. It is about life being lived as much more than mere survival and the attending to our bodily needs. Spirituality is about our communion with God, about our whole relationship with him, about our prayers to him, our worship of him, the exercise of any particular spiritual gifts that we, or indeed others, may feel that we have, all that we believe we must do in order to live full, satisfying lives in the world. Indeed, perhaps we may feel that we can say our spirituality is about our attempt, day by day and year by year to live in relationship with God—or perhaps "in fellowship" as at one time maybe commonly we called it. It could be said that for Christians spirituality is the fullness of their being human.

Nevertheless, we may experience a certain feeling that the Old Testament is hardly the correct and appropriate quarry to work in for finding help for the living of our lives in a spiritual relationship with God, for is there not in these documents a good deal that we perhaps should not take and seek to imitate, such as the violence we read about, certain examples of arrogance, some plainly unethical matters, the issue of appropriating lands and driving out earlier occupants? It cannot be denied that there are such issues and actions spoken about in these documents, and they do present some problems for contemporary Christians, and some of these issues will feature in the chapters which follow. Yet at the same time, such Old Testament problem passages by no means make up a large part of the Old Testament, and there are other aspects that surely do speak to us positively, and indeed of matters that we would wish to call "spiritual," as we shall see in what follows.

Thus, for example, when in the Old Testament book of Job the young man Elihu speaks he begins with a certain note of apology for making his contribution, for the reason that he is young, while those who have been dispensing their understandings of the ways of God with people in the world are so much senior to him and much more experienced at living life in the world. Yet Elihu believes that he does have something to contribute to the debate that is going on, that long debate we read about in the book of Job. So Elihu begins by asserting that there is something in a mortal that is nothing less than a gift of God, what is called "the spirit in a mortal," something from God that does nothing less than make for a certain understanding of the things of God on the part of that person. Elihu's words about this deserve to be quoted in full:

> But truly it is the spirit in a mortal,
>   the breath of the Almighty, that makes for understanding. (Job 32:8)

Some verses later Elihu will go on to say that it is the spirit of God that has made him what he is; it is the breath of the Almighty that continues to give him life (Job 33:4). It is surely this gift of God, this something, almost something of God himself, this "spirit of God," this "breath of the Almighty" that makes the human beings what they are, making them *both* human beings and *yet also* at the same time possessing something *spiritual* within them, thus enabling them to become spiritual beings—that is, coming to have, in the language of our contemporary times, a particular *spirituality* in and for their lives.

Yet it does still need to be said that our study of theology, our seeking to *understand* what we can of the ways of God, *and also* our associated
formulation of beliefs are both alike important to us in our speaking about
matters of spirituality. It is surely important that one of the principal sources
for the formulation of our spirituality is the study of theology, and that we
do thus seek to maintain a relationship between theology and spirituality.
Yet that having been said, we may be justified in observing that with certain
thinkers and writers about religious matters the boundaries between theology and spirituality are somewhat hazy, even difficult to define: what are we
to say what is theology, and what is spirituality? What, for example, would
we say about those two great works of Saint Augustine, his *Confessions* and
his *City of God*? Are they writings of and about theology, or are they in fact
works of spirituality? What shall we designate that well-known statement
of Augustine, "you have made us for yourself and our hearts find no peace
until they rest in you"? We *could* say that it is a theological statement; yet
it would perhaps be more accurate to say that it is about spirituality, for
it surely concerns our relationship with God, that spiritual relationship a
Christian feels, experiences, as Augustine expresses it, that stirs us deeply,
making us beings who are not content unless we are either praying for his
help or else praising him.

We may further observe that in some of the opening statements in the
books of Exodus and Deuteronomy we have something of this joining together of what we might possibly call theology and spirituality. In the words
of Deuteronomy cited at the head of this Introduction we have, "The LORD
is our God, the LORD alone. You shall love the LORD your God with all your
heart, and with all your soul, and with all your might" (Deut 6:4–5), while in
Exodus we read, "I am the LORD your God, who brought you out of the land
of Egypt, out of the house of slavery; you shall have no other gods before
me" (Exod 20:2–3). Yet each of these statements is about *both* theological
matters (in Deuteronomy "The LORD is our God . . ."; in Exodus "I am the
LORD your God . . .") and also about what we might wish to label spiritual
matters (in Deuteronomy "You shall love the LORD your God with all your
heart . . ." ; in Exodus "you shall have no other gods before me").

We should pause for a moment to consider that word "heart" which
occurs in the quotation above from Deut 6:5, for the Hebrew word for
"heart" does not mean quite what users of contemporary English mean by
it. The Hebrew, and therefore the Old Testament's, use of "heart" is not to
identify what keeps the blood flowing through the human body (they had
no knowledge of that; no-one did until the seventeenth century!), nor about
the expression of a thought or an action driven by emotion rather than by
strict logic. Rather, "heart" in Hebrew thought refers to the inner life of

an individual person, almost we might say that person's whole personality, their character. Indeed heart has been described by one Old Testament scholar thus: "It is the conscious and deliberate spiritual activity of the self-contained human ego which is meant . . ." This is not quite what we mean in our current Christian religious talk of "spirituality," but at the same time we can perhaps see that the Old Testament "heart" is not totally removed from it, but it is in fact speaking of an *aspect* of a person's inner spiritual being.

The present work is intended to make a modest contribution to the issue of what perhaps there is in the Old Testament—that is the Hebrew Bible—that treats matters, issues that appropriately and significantly add to and assist us in our search for a Christian spirituality for today. In the first place, however, it is perhaps necessary that some sort of case be made for bringing the Old Testament into the current debate about Christian spirituality, not least because in parts of the contemporary Christian Church in the western part of the world the Old Testament does not any longer appear to have a significant part to play. This may be owing to one, or both, of two considerations.

First, it may be asked what there is in the content of the Old Testament that may contribute to a contemporary Christian spirituality which we do not already have in the New Testament? Clearly the Old Testament documents come from a range of times and historical settings, a range of times that is in marked contrast to the comparatively short span of time from which the New Testament documents come. Thus there is truly what we might call a real sense in the Old Testament of Israel's faith being practiced in the various, and not-infrequently varied, settings in a whole range of historical eras and circumstances. While there might have been times such as those of kings David and Solomon when for the people of Israel a large degree of independence both in matters of religious practise and also of political direction were enjoyed, equally there were other times when there was a dominant external political power calling for a degree of faithfulness to its presence and role as Israel's overlord. Further there was also the historical reality of exile when many Israelites and their leaders were taken away into exile in distant lands, and forced to live under alien political rule and authority. This period of exile was a time when clearly questions were raised both about the presence or otherwise of their God with them in what at certain periods were searing events and troubled years. There was also the experience of a further change in circumstances for the people of Israel, this time with the possibility of returning to their homeland, though now under certain new circumstances as regards their neighbors and their political overlords.

We need to pause at this stage to take note of the word, this name, *Israel* in the expression "Israel's faith" used in the preceding paragraph, because in the Old Testament this name is used in two main ways. In Genesis 32:28 "Israel" is the new name that Jacob receives, and that is the name generally given to the descendants of Jacob, "the people of Israel." Further, in Canaan they are spoken of as living in the land of Israel. However after the death of the Israelite King Solomon the Israelite nation became divided, the tribe of Judah remaining loyal to Solomon's son Rehoboam and becoming known as the tribe of Judah, living in the land of Judah with their capital city of Jerusalem, while the remainder of the tribes transferred their loyalty to Jeroboam, living in northern Israel, becoming generally known as the Northern Kingdom of Israel, or simply Israel, and establishing main centers in both Dan in the north and Bethel in the south.

There is thus behind, providing the worldly backdrop as it were to, certain of the Old Testament documents and books the reflection of a real sense of change, perhaps this being at times for some of the people involved a meaningful experience of development and advance, while no doubt for others there would be a feeling of this being rather a change for the worse. These political changes and experiences brought about certain inevitable changes in religious practices, and even in religious beliefs, and such are reflected in certain parts of the Old Testament. Thus there is in our Old Testament documents what I have called this whole matter of an ongoing experience of life in all its changes, variations, setbacks, and also advances. This is something we find in the Old Testament, which because of its sheer historical span and "length" is not found in the New Testament, by comparison a collection of documents that come from a much more restricted time span.

We should also perhaps take note of the fact that in the Old Testament there is a very considerable emphasis on—along with documents about—worship, and again certain changes in these matters took place as historical circumstances changed. Moreover, as regards worship there is expressed in the pages of the Old Testament a real sense of the greatness and otherness, the sheer and sometimes overwhelming awesomeness and holiness of the Lord God, perhaps accompanied by a profound sense of failure and sinfulness on the part of those who are coming to worship him. Thus there is much here both about de-sinning rites for those who would come before their Lord, and further in the book of Psalms a remarkable and varied collection of expressions of divine praise and seeking for human beings to make in a wide range of settings, moods and experiences.

The second consideration that may bring about a certain reluctance on the part of some Christians to turn to the Old Testament must be those scenes of conflict and violence we come across in this part of the Bible, no small number of these being portrayed as having been initiated by the Lord, or at least taking place with his approval. How can such things be happening with the approval of the Lord who in the New Testament, and in many other parts of the Old, can be portrayed as loving and caring? Further, how can such gruesome accounts be regarded as parts of inspired scripture? There are undoubtedly such problematical parts of the Old Testament, and some of these are discussed in the chapter below on Ethical concerns. Yet the continuing difficulties in these matters tend to stand revealed in no small way as they are used in the services and liturgies of the Church. Perhaps we have to accept that these are aspects of how ancient peoples did sometimes express their belief that their Lord God did truly care for them, guide and protect them, even in the hurly-burly of the clash of the nations, and the warlike aspirations of their neighbors. However, it should be noted that here we are talking about only *some* parts of the Old Testament, and that we should not magnify their occurrences and the occasional somewhat grue-some accounts, and thereby neglect the reality that there is so much else in the Hebrew Bible, in particular matters that are deeply challenging, or reassuring, and all those various words and stories that are intended to set forth visions and portrayals of a loving, caring, guiding, and delivering God.

Further, there is a certain perception on the part of some less-than-enthusiastic readers of the Old Testament that here is material that is now out of date, even somewhat redundant. That is to say, now that we have the later revelation of the Lord through Christ—and even more that we live in the age of the Holy Spirit—do those who live in the New Testament era really need to read and use the records, documents, and writings from the earlier eras? That is to say, now that we live in the time of Christ in the age of *grace*, do we need to consider matters relating to *law* in the Old Testament? Yet the fact is surely that there are *both* law and grace in *both* the Old and the New Testaments, and further that Christians surely need to hear, and be challenged by, the words about law and about grace in them *both*. Moreover, there is much in the Old Testament about a people who for various reasons live in a series of "ages," or eras, that is a people who are forced to experience change in their individual and corporate lives, many-a-time unwillingly, but nevertheless compelled by apparently worldly circumstances, to live in change. The Old Testament in its various documents bears witness to such matters, and further makes its witness to the struggles of both leaders and people to deal with those issues. And there again is surely material and help, as well as challenge, for those who in their contemporary settings seek to live out an appropriate Christian spirituality, in particular in times of change and upheaval.

Yet there are other matters that may cause offence to Christians in the twenty-first century, such as the fact that for so much of the time the address of the Lord to the humans—and this is not alone in the Old Testament but is also there in the New—is in fact to *men* rather than to *women and men*. Nevertheless the Hebrew word for "man" does occur often without specific reference to gender, and thus the New Revised Standard Version of the Bible usually changes the traditional translation *men* to *men and women*, which does concur with many of our current conventions and practices. Yet the Bible in all its various parts did come so frequently from a male-dominated and largely male-led society, and all too often speaks of the male-like strength of the Lord in his worldly creations and dealings. Further within these ancient documents that make-up the Bible, no doubt in particular in the Old Testament, there are parts that cause us real difficulties such as, for example, the treatment meted out to certain female captives as spoken about in Deut 21:10–14. Such matters do pose difficulties for many contemporary Christians. And perhaps all that we can do is to recall the fact that we are indeed reading and dealing with documents that came from long ago, and moreover from societies and cultures that were very different from those of our contemporary world—or at least from particular parts of the contemporary world.

Yet at the same time we perhaps need to recall and come to terms with that sense of *earthiness* about so much in the Old Testament, insofar as it is considerably occupied with the living-out of a religious faith in the settings of worldly life and human circumstances. The sheer fact that the Old Testament presents to us a people whose history was punctuated by changes and other challenges that we have observed, may be of considerable help and significance for Christians who themselves go through change, and whose churches may thus also have to undergo development and adaptation. There must surely be benefit for those in the Christian Church to hear about the experiences of their predecessors in faith, and how they reacted and adapted to their own developing circumstances.

On the other hand, in spite of various problematical parts of the Old Testament such as those mentioned above, there is also much material in other parts of it that are deeply treasured in the Christian Church. The Book of Psalms is regarded by so many Christians as a great well of material for public worship and private meditation, and within that large collection of psalms, how greatly, for example, is the twenty-third psalm treasured. Then, so many of the biblical psalms are shot full of expressions of a person's relationship with the Lord—as for example we read in Ps 4:1 "You gave me room when I was in distress"; in Ps 7:1 "O LORD my God, in you I take refuge"; in Ps 9:12 "he does not forget the cry of the afflicted"; in Ps 16:11

"You show me the path of life. In your presence there is fullness of joy; in your right hand are pleasures for evermore", and so on.

The book of Isaiah is widely employed in Christian lectionaries, and so is much else in the books of the prophets, in the book of Psalms and elsewhere in the Old Testament. In fact, what follows in this modest work is intended to argue that the Church has much to gain from a caring and careful attention to the Old Testament, for in spite of parts of those documents presenting difficulties, even embarrassments, to Christians, there is surely much else—indeed surely far more!—that is of untold benefit to us, that is in fact needed in our search for an appropriate spirituality for the days in which we live, and that should surely be heard in the Church today.

Above all, there are some parts of the Old Testament that for Christians have words full of meaning and significance, such words by no means being rendered out of date, or inappropriate, in the light of the New Testament and its message that "the Word became flesh and lived among us, and we have seen his glory, the glory as of a father's only son, full of grace and truth." (John 1:14) For surely those very early-occurring words of the Old Testament about the singularly privileged place of humankind in the world is still as appropriate as ever, as challenging as ever, namely, "Then God said, 'Let us make humankind in our image, according to our likeness . . .'" (Gen 1:26), and, "then the LORD God formed man from the dust of the ground, and breathed into his nostrils the breath of life, and the man became a living being." (Gen 2:7) That latter word is surely intended to say metaphorically something to the reader about a divinely-given and singularly privileged place of fellowship between the humans and the Lord of the world and creation, the whole matter which in our own day we are tending to designate as our spiritual relationship with God—our spirituality. Thus too do Christians find meaning and significance in those ancient words of the psalmist,

> When I look at your heavens, the work of your fingers,
>   the moon and the stars that you have established;
> what are human beings that you are mindful of them,
>   mortals that you care for them?
> Yet you have made them a little lower than God,
>   and crowned them with glory and honor. (Ps 8:3–5)

How remarkably bold is this thought of the psalmist, picturing the human beings in such a close and privileged relationship with their divine Lord. Perhaps it is not totally surprising that the words of the Hebrew about the humans being divinely made "a little lower than God" was too much, being hardly sufficiently reverential to the divine, for those translators who in rendering it into the Greek substituted "than the angels" for the Hebrew

version's "than God." Yet the Hebrew Bible does truly speak about a remarkable closeness of the Lord of the world to his people, and that in spite of
ongoing human sinfulness and failures he remains committed to them, and
accepts them "warts and all." Thus we also read in the Old Testament,

> Who is a God like you, pardoning iniquity
> and passing over the transgression
> of the remnant of your possession?
> He does not retain his anger forever,
> because he delights in showing clemency.
> He will again have compassion upon us;
> he will tread our iniquities under foot.
> You will cast all our sins
> into the depths of the sea.
> You will show faithfulness to Jacob
> and unswerving loyalty to Abraham,
> as you have sworn to our ancestors
> from the days of old. (Mic 7:18–20)

Or we may speak about just a few of those many examples occurring
in the Old Testament in which it is made abundantly clear that there is a
real and spiritual relationship between the Lord and individuals on earth.
As we shall come to see in the chapter below on what there is in the Old
Testament about worship, these scriptures have much to say about prayer,
for with considerable frequency they portray various people as praying to
the Lord, and of their Lord's hearing them. We shall also see in that same
chapter the sense of lively awareness that the making of offerings and sacrifices to the Lord is believed to be truly pleasing to the Lord. Further, there
are a considerable number of examples in the Hebrew Bible of individuals
who are confronted with the Lord—such as Moses on a mountain being
called to service (Exod 3:1–22); Elijah, again on a mountain, seeking a sense
of reassurance in the midst of his prophetic ministry (1 Kgs 19:1–18); of a
woman named Hannah praying in a sanctuary with deep intensity for the
gift of a child (1 Sam 1:3–28). Not infrequently the call narrative of certain
individuals to prophetic service demonstrates the reality of such spiritual
relationships. Further, such narratives show belief in the Lord's need to have
people on earth who through such spiritual relationships with himself will
be used to foster both individual and also national relationships between
the humans and the divine one (see for example Isa 1:16–17; Amos 5:21–24;
Mic 6:8).

Here and in so many other places in the Old Testament is an implied
possibility of a closeness of relationship between an individual and the Lord.

That is, an individual who lives the life of earth can yet and at the same time also have a relationship with the Lord, a spiritual relationship with him, that those of earth can have an "inner life," an "interior life" of fellowship with God. We may perhaps go further than this, being more specific about this "inner life," saying that the Old Testament portrays us as having been made "spiritual beings," those who have relationships not only with others of their humanity, but who can also be in fellowship with the Lord, that is have a spiritual relationship with the divine and holy One, and thus live lives of spirituality. Indeed, perhaps something of the very heart of this matter is expressed in the closing words of the forty-sixth psalm:

> "Be still, and know that I am God!
> I am exalted among the nations,
> I am exalted in the earth."
> The LORD of hosts is with us;
> the God of Jacob is our refuge. (Ps 46:10–11)

Here is emphasized both the greatness of the God of the world, and at the same time his closeness with the individuals and the communities of his people.

How shall we go about organizing this attempt to set forth something of what the Old Testament has perhaps to contribute to a contemporary Christian spirituality for today? For while the Old Testament may have a particular way in which it is organized, that is perhaps not the way we would wish the material to be set forth for *our* purposes, in the context of what is hopefully a contribution to the living out of a Christian spirituality in the twenty-first century. What arrangement of this Old Testament material will suit our purposes, one that goes at least some way towards setting forth what we believe is there in its documents for the fashioning of a contemporary spirituality for Christians? After this brief introduction to the work, I offer a series of chapters, in each of which I seek to highlight and set forth various emphases found in the Hebrew Bible which I believe contribute significantly, maybe in some instances even vitally, to our contemporary Christian spirituality.

However, it does have to be said that in the following treatment there are inevitably some repetitions in our attention to a number of Old Testament themes. This is because, quite simply, any attempt at a thematic treatment of the biblical material is not, of course, in the arrangement we find in the Old Testament itself. Thus I ask for the understanding and patience of my readers, who may be feeling that surely we have already considered what, for instance, a certain prophet had to say on this or that subject.

Each of the chapters below bears the word "Life" in its title, for I intend that there shall be an emphasis in this work on the *living out* of religious faith—which as I understand the matter is what "spirituality" as it is currently spoken about is concerned with—and thus Chapter 1 is entitled "Life in Creation and Covenant." In that chapter I speak about the God who is at the center of the Old Testament documents, the God to whom those documents continually call people back, reminding them of his gracious creation of and provision for them, inviting them into, or perhaps back into, lives of spiritual relationship with him, and at the same time of his ongoing call to them to worship him, to follow him faithfully, and to serve him in their earthly lives. The word used in the Old Testament for this relationship of God and his people is "Covenant."

Chapter 2, "Life with Deliverance and Judgment," is about the two aspects of the deliverance and the judgment of the Lord, that he both cares deeply for his people and their worldly circumstances, and yet at the same time does not turn a "blind eye" to their sinful acts and lives, but intends rather that we live our lives focussed on him and his purposes. In this chapter we need to grapple with what some contemporary people regard as a somewhat harsh judgmental God spoken about in certain of the pages of the Old Testament.

Chapter 3 is entitled "Life of Worship," for there is indeed much in the Old Testament about worship, not only in the book of Psalms, but in fact, as we shall see, in one way or another in most of the books that make up the whole of the Old Testament scriptures. Here in these parts of the Old Testament about the worship of God is surely the call to individuals and communities to live out their earthly lives in a conscious spiritual relationship of prayer and praise with their Lord.

Chapter 4, "Life in Community," seeks to bring out one of the central emphases of the Old Testament, namely that as well as the individual there is the community, and that individuals both in the world and the Church do need the reality of their membership of and part in communities. Thus the Old Testament speaks of the importance of human caring, in particular of the call to care for those whose lives are difficult, for those who are in distress or who are dispossessed, as is for example expressed in much detail and broadness in the book of Deuteronomy (see Deut 22:1–30). In this chapter there is consideration of the ministries of prophets, priests, and kings.

Chapter 5, "Life in a Changing World," is about what these days would be referred to as the political settings and surroundings of the lives of the people of God. The spiritual life is to be lived out in such settings, perhaps in a national community, and the Old Testament speaks about the change and decay it so often observes in the contemporary community of the faithful, and about the national grappling to find appropriate ways for its political leadership to exercise both care and purpose, and to secure a worthy place in the life of the peoples of the world—and all this moreover when that world is not infrequently undergoing changes. Indeed, it may well be that our own spiritual lives are to be lived out in company with, and perhaps some understanding of, those of other spiritualities than our own, and certainly also in days of change. Further reference will be made here to the ministries and preaching of some of the great Hebrew prophets, and to some of their bold words in seeking to interpret the ways of God to his people, when those people were apparently being buffeted around, even as we might say, being plagued by more politically powerful nations around them. In such interventions by the surrounding nations great political and social changes were liable to be effected upon the peoples of Judah and Israel.

Chapter 6, "Life with Questions," is concerned with the theological grappling we witness in parts of the Old Testament concerning questions about suffering on the part of apparently righteous people. These are some of the difficult issues which have been labelled "theodicy questions," that is, questions about the justice of God: if God is righteous and loving, why do so many apparently righteous people experience suffering in the world? In this chapter we consider in particular the books of Job and Ecclesiastes, but also attend to some of the psalms, that is to some of the so-called "Wisdom Psalms," and to parts of the book of Jeremiah.

Chapter 7, "Life with Ethical Concerns," is about the people of God being called to live life with a real emphasis on care and concern for others, that is to espouse a series of ethical concerns. There are, it does have to be said, a number of problems and issues to be faced in looking to the Old Testament in this regard, for clearly, as already observed, a number of quite seriously *unethical* ways of the people of Israel are spoken about in these scriptures, and these parts of the Old Testament inevitably demand a certain critical attention on our part. Chapter 8, "Life with a Future," concerns what we find in the Old Testament about possibilities for the future for those who live on earth, not only as individuals, but also for their nation, and further for the world in which they live. We also ask in this chapter what expressions of hope are to be found in the Hebrew Bible about a life after earthly death.

Each of these chapters, after this present Introductory one, concludes with a section entitled "From Texts to Spirituality," and here I try to suggest ways in which the preceding material in that chapter does, so I believe, have some particular and appropriate application in the fashioning and possible formation of a Christian spirituality. I endeavor here to ensure that my material is not just left in the field of Old Testament study, but that at least some parts of it do have contributions to make to the pursuit of spirituality, and the living of the spiritual life, in the world of today. Sometimes this section includes a quotation or other contribution from a writing on Christian spirituality.

Chapter 9 is the concluding chapter in which I seek to draw together some threads of the above studies, and to gather up some possible conclusions and consequences of this study of the Old Testament for the fashioning and pursuit of the life of Christian spirituality in the world of the twenty-first century. We finish with some brief guidance on possible further reading on the topics and aspects covered by the various chapters of the book.

In that study, now acknowledged as a classic of Christian spirituality, *Revelations of Divine Love*, the author, Julian of Norwich, says in one place that there are four kinds of goodness that God offers us, as follows:

> It is his wish that we should have knowledge of four things: the first is that he is the ground from which we have all our life and our being; the second, that he protects us mightily and mercifully in the time of our sin and among all the enemies that fall upon us so fiercely . . . the third is that he protects us with kind courtesy and lets us know that we are going wrong; the fourth is how steadfastly he waits for us with unchanging face, for he wants us to turn to him and unite with him in love, as he is united with us.

I trust that the following treatment of parts of the Old Testament affirms that the Hebrew Bible does indeed amongst much else bear its witness to this same goodness that God offers us, and to a good deal else besides. And with that we may proceed to the first of our chosen topics, namely what the Old Testament has to say to us about Life in Creation and Covenant, that is life in relationships with both the Lord and also with others of his people on earth.

1

Life in Creation and Covenant

> In the year that King Uzziah died, I saw the LORD sitting on a
> throne, high and lofty; and the hem of his robe filled the temple.
> Seraphs were in attendance above him; each had six wings: with
> two they covered their faces, and with two they covered their
> feet, and with two they flew. And one called to another and said:
> "Holy, holy, holy is the LORD of hosts;
> The whole earth is full of his glory." (Isa 6:1–3)

THESE SUBLIME WORDS FROM the sixth chapter of the book of Isaiah set
forth something—indeed, perhaps as much as can be expressed in mere
words—of the overwhelming experience of the prophet concerning the
holy, and totally other, Lord, an experience which he had in what sounds
like the Jerusalem temple. While this particular part of the Old Testament
may be in something of a class all of its own for its expressions of the holiness, the majesty and sheer glory of this God, yet his divine presence and
activity in the world, and in particular his involvement in the individual
and corporate lives of his people, are acknowledged, portrayed, and spoken
about throughout the books of the Old Testament.

The Old Testament portrays this God as always having been present
with his creation, indeed that he was the one who both willed the creation
of the world and also effected it (see Gen 1:1—2:25). Further, Psalm 90:1–2
affirms, "Lord, you have been our dwelling place in all generations. Before
the mountains were brought forth, or ever you had formed the earth and the
world, from everlasting to everlasting you are God." Moreover, the words of
that psalm about the everlasting nature and activity of the Lord are reflected

in some of the speech and language of the book of Isaiah chapters 40–55, "I am the first and I am the last; besides me there is no god." (Isa 44:6. See also Isa 40:28; 41:4)

Yet further, what we have in many of the books of the Old Testament is this God portrayed as having a covenant relationship with his people Israel. That is, the Lord established a special relationship between himself and his people Israel in which for both parties there would be commitment each to the other; for his part the Lord would be the Guide and Guardian of his people, while for their part the people would acknowledge this Lord God as their sole and unchallenged God, and seek to be obedient to him and his commands, going in the ways of life that he prescribes—expressed for example in such formulations as the Ten Commandments (Exod 20:1–17; Deut 5:6–21). Thus were the people Israel in a particular relationship with the Lord, a relationship both beneficial and demanding for those people.

This covenant God is named Yahweh, this sometimes being shortened to Yah, as in certain human names, such as Eli-jah, Jerem-iah , and as in the word of praise "Hallelu-jah" ("Praise Yah"). Sometime before the end of the Old Testament period this name came to be regarded as possessed of such a degree of holiness which rendered it advisable not to be audibly spoken, and thus in reading and speaking coming to be substituted by the alternative Adonay, meaning "My Lord." The result was that in the reading of a text one would *read* Yahweh, but would *say* instead Adonay.

It was believed that there was something most special about Israel's God, something awesome about him, something that to a certain extent is even to be called "frightening" about him. This is spoken about in the Isaiah ch 6 account of the experience of the prophet in the temple, though the actual words "holy" are portrayed as being uttered by the seraphs, that is semi-divine beings whose dwelling place is spoken of as being closer to the presence of the holy than could be essayed or even contemplated by any human person. Yet there is something of the holy one, the "other" one, the deity, that can be seen, glimpsed on earth, and that is his "glory." Perhaps there is indeed in that word, and in the experience of glimpsing, experiencing this sense of "glory" something of that holiness of the Lord that can on occasions be seen, perhaps sometimes no more than glimpsed, on earth, yet what for so much of the time appears to elude human experience. Nevertheless, what can be perceived on earth of this burning holiness of God, by the inevitably limited human sensibilities, is perhaps this sense of "glory," this experience from time to time, for many people of earth maybe only on infrequent occasions, a tiny revelation of a little of the otherwise "unseeable."

As if to reinforce the point about the vast difference there is between the human beings and the divine one, Israel's God, the Lord Yahweh, we are told in a range of parts of the Old Testament that the Lord Yahweh is surrounded by what is portrayed as something in the nature of a heavenly "court." Thus we read in Ps 82:1,

> God has taken his place in the divine council;
> in the midst of the gods he holds judgment . . .

However, it is not indicated or even suggested that these "gods" have any divine powers. Perhaps what is being expressed here is that Yahweh, the greatest of all divinities, is surrounded by members of his "divine council," some of those who appear to be members thereof being spoken about elsewhere. In 1 Kgs 6–8 and in Ezek 10 we have a considerable number of references to *cherubim*, and these seem to have been imagined hybrid creatures, frequently represented as winged sphinxes, and perhaps thought of as guarding the deity on his heavenly throne. Further, there are *seraphim*, though only appearing in Isa 6:2–3. Again, these are winged creatures. Moreover, there are "angels," though these could be actual members of the divine court, or else the deity's messengers, or even Yahweh himself. Yet they are spoken of not infrequently in the Old Testament, in particular in Genesis, Judges, and Zechariah 1–6, and sometimes the Lord may speak through an angel—see, for example Gen 18:1—19:5. Nor should we neglect to mention the portrayal of "The Satan" in the opening two chapters of the book of Job and elsewhere. In Job 1 and 2 this figure is identified as one of "the sons of God," suggesting that he is indeed a member of the Lord's heavenly court. See also 1 Chr 21:1. Thus does the Old Testament portray the greatness of the Lord Yahweh, and indeed his surpassing greatness over all other divinities.

The Old Testament begins with two narratives that speak about the Lord's work in his creation of the world and the people who live in it. Both of these accounts stand very much on their own, without any serious parallels in the Bible. Yet first we need to ask: what sort of material is this, and how are we intended to read it? Is it what we today would call a history of the world, in which first this was made, and then something else? The fact that there are two "accounts" (Gen 1:1—2:4a and 2:4b–25), and further that they are very different treatments, having different emphases and concerns, would surely suggest that they cannot both be correct "historically." The viewpoint taken in this present work is that these accounts are hardly "historical" pieces that are to understood literally, but rather that their emphasis is intended to be upon the perceived will, the purposes, the designs of the world and the human beings willed by the Lord God. One recent commentator on these chapters speaks about our "listening to a song of creation," and while some of my readers will understand these accounts "historically,"

I for my part am well content to read their poetic language as presenting us with two particular songs of and about God's good creation.

The first account, found in Gen 1:1—2:4a, portrays the creation of the whole wide scene of the world, and makes clear in its opening words that this is the work of none other than the Lord God, who is generally referred to here as "God," as expressed in the first words of the Old Testament—and the whole Bible: "In the beginning when God created the heavens and the earth" (Gen 1:1). Out of what had been a formless void God created the heavens and the earth, and behind the apparent simplicity of the language employed to express these amazing statements, there is surely on the part of the careful and sympathetic reader an imagined sense of awe and won-der—that nothing less than the created heavens and earth should have been brought out of what had been darkness and a formless void. That sense of awe is present as the account continues with what is portrayed as having been done on the first day,

> Then God said, "Let there be light"; and there was light. And God saw that the light was good; and God separated the light from the darkness. God called the light Day, and the darkness he called Night. And there was evening and there was morning, the first day. (Gen 1:3–5)

With the words here "God saw that the light was good" (1:4) we have the first of a series of seven such expressions concerning the divine work of creation. What is expressed as the pleasure of God in his work of creation, is both an affirmation of the goodness of the created world for all future generations, and also as a source of human awe and wonder at the creative and creating work of the Creator. Such a sense of holy awe at this work of divine creation is powerfully expressed in the opening of the first of the two speeches of the Lord to the questioning, and complaining, man named Job:

> Where were you when I laid the foundation of the earth?
> Tell me, if you have understanding.
> Who determined its measurements—surely you know!
> Or who stretched the line upon it?
> On what were its bases sunk,
> or who laid its cornerstone
> when the morning stars sang together
> and all the heavenly beings shouted for joy? (Job 38:4–7)

Or we might be quoting from Psalm 93:

> The LORD is king, he is robed in majesty;
> the LORD is robed, he is girded with strength.

He has established the world; it shall never be moved;
your throne is established from of old;
you are from everlasting. (Ps 93:1–2)

So this account of the creation of the world continues: on the second day with the creation of the sky and the separation of the waters above it, from those below it (Gen 1:6–8); on the third day with the establishment of the earth, the sea, and vegetation (1:9–13); on the fourth day the creation of the great lights, the sun and the moon (1:14–19); on the fifth day the creation of the living creatures, the birds, the sea monsters (1:20–23); and finally on the sixth day the creation not only of the living creatures, cattle, creeping things, wild animals (1:24–25) but also of humanity, according we are told, to the divine likeness, and with dominion over the fishes, the birds, cattle and wild animals, not forgetting those creeping things that creep upon the earth:

> Then God said, "Let us make humankind in our image, according to our likeness; and let them have dominion over the fish of the sea, and over the birds of the air, and over the cattle, and over all the wild animals of the earth, and over every creeping thing that creeps upon the earth." (Gen 1:26)

This calls for a number of comments. In the first place there is a sense here that humankind has been put in a place of responsibility in the creation, in particular under God being responsible for fish, birds, animals and those beings that creep on the earth. None other, and no others, in this account of the divine creation are spoken about in such terms of human responsibility. But then, these humans have been made to have a particular relationship with the Lord, having been made in his "image," in his "likeness." In all probability we should not look for different meanings for these two words, "image" and "likeness"; it is very probable that the writer is using that common ploy of the Hebraic writers to express the matter, and then further to express it using a different word, a procedure we know well from the book of Psalms (see, for example, Pss 2:8, 9; 3:1; 4:7; 5:4 and so on).

What, however, would seem to be of greater significance here is the sense of relationship expressed between the Lord and the humans, whether that be through word "image" or whether through "likeness." What is surely being emphasized here is the sense of comparative closeness of the humans to God, that is in comparison with any other of the creatures and living beings. The Old Testament commentator Claus Westermann said of these words, "The relationship to God is not something which is added to human existence; humans are created in such a way that their very existence is intended to be their relationship to God." Further, this matter of the creation of the humans is given more extended treatment than the preceding details of other parts of the creation, clearly being placed at this stage in the account so as to give a real sense of this being the climax, the crown, the final glory of the creation, for the writer continues,

> So God created humankind in his image,
>   in the image of God he created them;
>   male and female he created them.
> God blessed them, and God said to them, "Be fruitful and multiply, and fill the earth and subdue it; and have dominion over the fish of the sea and over the birds of the air and over every living thing that moves upon the earth." (Gen 1:27–28)

What is being said here is that some particular gifts have been given to the humans to relate to God, in particular to relate to him in a way and to a depth that is not given to the other creatures spoken about in Gen 1:1—2:4a. We may say, surely not unreasonably, that these verses do speak of what has come to be referred to as the humans being given the opportunity and privilege of what we might call a spiritual relationship with God. There is here something that has been gathered into the sense of what has come to be called "spirituality," the human beings are portrayed as intended to be in relationship with the Lord, to live their lives in relationship with him, interacting with him and his purposes, having—or at least being able to have—a *spiritual* relationship with him.

When completed, all these great works of the Lord appeared to the Lord to be "indeed . . . very good" (Gen 1:31), and we are told something solemn about this day, this seventh day. For perhaps not quite all had been created, and on this seventh day we are told the Lord rested, blessing and hallowing all that he had done and created, so creating also rest and resting. This does indeed set forth and present to us a sense of the great power and goodness of the Creator, and at the same time that of the particular relationship of the divine and holy one with his created human beings.

This account of creation in Gen 1:1—2:4a is followed in 2:4b–25 by what is apparently a second account. This, however, is very different from what precedes, for in particular it is restricted in its concern with just one part of the divine creation, namely the creation of the human beings, the creation of the man and of the woman. There are certain aspects of this account of which we should take note in the context of this study of the Old Testament and Christian spirituality. Here it is once again stressed that in the creation of the man there is portrayed something of a special relationship engendered in the created man by the creating God: "Then the LORD

God formed man from the dust of the ground, and breathed into his nostrils the breath of life; and the man became a living being." (Gen 2:7) Such words of intimacy between the Creator and the created are not used in the Old Testament elsewhere, but rather only here in these accounts of the creation. But then this man, this Adam, is portrayed as the human father of all who will come after him, so that we may speak once again of a real closeness of relationship between this first man and the Lord God, and thereby through the bearing of descendants by Adam and his partner and helper (2:18–25) future generations may/will come into this life of relationship with the Lord. Further, as many parts of the Old Testament understand the matter, at death this "breath" returns to God, the individual having been "created" when the Lord sends forth his breath (NRSV "spirit") (Ps 104:29–30). Yet for his life on earth Adam is indeed a "living being." Adam had received the very "breath of God" into his life, thus surely again being portrayed as living in a "spiritual" relationship with God. Adam was indeed human, yet also he was "spirited," made a spiritual person, one for whom life is portrayed as intended from his very creation to be one of "spirituality."

So we come to Genesis chapter 3, where we find talk of "the serpent." We are told, "Now the serpent was more crafty than any other wild animal that the LORD God had made. He said to the woman, 'Did God say, "You shall not eat from any tree in the garden"?'" (Gen 3:1) For indeed the serpent was portrayed as being crafty—seriously crafty—in fact coming later to stand for Satan. Yet already there appears to be a certain demonic power in the serpent, one whose crafty moves and words made it a challenge to the authority of the Lord, who although spoken about as if having been created by God (Gen 3:1), yet is also presented as being "anti-God." Indeed, the serpent seems to be anti-God, embodying those forces, tendencies, aspirations that go against the will and purposes of the Lord God. He is the one who tempts the humans to go against God's instructions, suggesting that they eat some of that divinely-forbidden fruit in the center of the garden, that fruit growing on the "tree of life" (Gen 3:1–7, 22). In effect this story in Gen 3 invites us to become aware of sin, and all that tendency that the human beings know only so very well to rebel against God and his ways. And this is a indeed a fearful and ever-tempting tendency, which truly is so very remarkably represented in the creation story by the antics of that slithery, sliding-around serpent, with dreadfully beguiling words.

So we read at the end of Genesis ch 3 about a certain change in status of the human beings and of their banishment from the paradise garden:

> Therefore the LORD God sent him [the man] forth from the
> garden of Eden, to till the ground from which he was taken.

> He drove out the man; and at the east of the garden of Eden he
> placed the cherubim, and a sword flaming and turning to guard
> the way to the tree of life. (Gen 3:23–24)

This ancient story, with all its graphic imagery of a speaking serpent is about the reality in the world of sin. That is, what God has called his people to do, and what not to do, mysteriously presents his people—and this is all people in all ages—with the strongest of temptations to speak and act in contrary ways.

Yet the Old Testament continues to speak of the human beings as those who are privileged and called to have a relationship of closeness to the Lord, in a particular way through its talk of a series of covenants: "covenant," as we have seen, being one of the characteristic words of the Bible whereby the particular, indeed special, relationship between God and his people is indicated. Thus Deuteronomy expresses the matter,

> For you are a people holy to the Lord your God; it is you the
> Lord has chosen out of all the peoples on earth to be his people,
> his treasured possession. (Deut 14:2)

The people of Israel are described here—and also in virtually the same words in Deut 7:6—as being a people set apart for God and to be involved in God's purposes; they have been chosen by the Lord to be in the nature of his own treasured possession. Presumably the thought must be that God intends that these people shall be his chosen people, those who will look to him for the very sources of their lives, who will live in ways acceptable to him, and who will do his will in the world. No doubt, while the expression "holy to the Lord" carries with it the sense of the people of Israel being called to shun evil ways, and anything else that is opposed to the will and way of God, perhaps rather its primary intended sense is that these people are to live in ways that accord with the Lord's holy will, so that they reflect something of his love and care for them.

In these divinely instituted covenants the Lord for his part will care for and guide his people, while they will live for him, obey his commands, and seek to live out the divinely prescribed standards of morals and ethical living. The covenant is above all about relationships, in particular and in view of the fact that the major partner in this covenant is a Being who is certainly real—but who is yet invisible, untouchable, mysterious; close at hand and yet at the same time far away—it is a relationship of manifest unequals. The instituting of any such covenant is also inevitably from the divine side, yet here in the Old Testament are various accounts of this God establishing covenants with his people, each of them with various differences, adapted so to speak to new and emerging situations and concerns. Yet within each and all of them are the basic themes of the divine protection and guidance on the one hand, and of the human faithfulness and obedience on the other.

The first covenant spoken about in the Old Testament concerns Noah, and the major happening of the flood and the associated building of the ark; in fact the narrative of this whole incident (Gen 6:9—9:28) both begins with and ends with references to God's covenant with his people: in Gen 6:18 God making a covenant with Noah and all his family, at the end in Gen 9:16 with God making a covenant with "every living creature of all flesh that is on the earth." Yet even within the book of Genesis there are accounts of further covenants: God makes a covenant with Abram (Gen 15:18; 17:1–14); there is covenant agreement between Abraham and Abimelech (21:27–31); later one between Isaac and Abimelech (26:28–31), not forgetting the one between Jacob and Laban (31:44–54). Here are members of family, even of tribal groups who make solemn commitments to and with the Lord in regard to faithful service on the one hand, and protection, guidance, love and care on the other hand. In the first two cases mentioned above it is the Lord God and Abram who are the covenant parties.

However, the covenant spoken about in the book of Exodus, which was concluded in the period of the sojourn in the desert, in particular at the foot of Mount Sinai, following on from the escape of the Israelite slaves from Egypt, is a covenant made with the whole people of Israel. Here the giving of the commandments and much else, is spoken about in very considerable detail, surely indicating a particularly significant covenant making/renewing. This therefore calls for rather more extended treatment.

The fact that the people are there in the desert at the foot of the mountain is witness to the believed reality that the Lord was, indeed had actually been, the delivering God of the people of Israel. The Lord had heard the cries of distress of his people in their slave-laboring in Egypt, and it was he—none other than their Lord and God—who had brought them out of Egypt and led them safely across the waters. All this, we are told, was in the armed presence of the Egyptian army that had been sent by the Pharaoh with orders to stop them (Exod 14:1–31). Thus the people "feared" the Lord, that is, as we might say, "reverenced" him, were "in awe of" him (the same Hebrew word is used for both "fear" and "revere"). Through the experience of having been delivered, the people believed in the Lord and in his servant Moses, they engaged in the singing of songs of praise, thus extolling their delivering Lord (Exod 15:1–18a, 20–21). Through such deliverances did Moses and the people, in spite of various problems and shortages on the way—from which once again the Lord is said to have delivered them as a result of their crying out to him in distress (see Exod 16:1—18:27)—arrive at the foot of Mount Sinai (Exod 19:1).

There is a sense in which the basic story-line of Israel's desert travels stops here, for the rest of what Exodus records concerns the relationship of the Lord God and his people (Exod 19:1—40:38). This relationship is expressed once again in the terminology of covenant, which the Lord offers to his people, the central features being that those people agree to the Ten Commandments in their serving the Lord, while the Lord for his part will guard and guide them through their individual and corporate lives (Exod 19:1—24:18). Then in a large block of material details about places of worship are set out (Exod 25:1—31:18); we hear about Israelite sinfulness in their manufacture of the "golden calf," the people's worship of it and their asking it to lead them on through the desert (32:1—33:23); of the subsequent renewal of the covenant relationship (34:1–35); and about the building of the already-detailed sanctuary (35:1—40:38). These are central matters in this study of the Old Testament and Christian spirituality, and call for further fleshing out.

Exodus 19:1—24:18 concerns the relationship between the Lord Yahweh and his people Israel, and is expressed in the Old Testament's characteristic language of "covenant," in which the Lord's part will be to guard, guide, direct, deliver his people, while they for their part are required to be faithful to him, be obedient to his commands, and live out those expressions of his requirements to them, in particular that is to the Ten Commandments (20:1–21). The fundamentals of the covenant may be said to be expressed in Exod 19:5–6a, which reads,

> Now therefore, if you obey my voice and keep my covenant, you shall be my treasured possession out of all the peoples. Indeed, the whole earth is mine, but you shall be for me a priestly kingdom and a holy nation.

To be noticed here is the special relationship that Israel is to have with its God (a "treasured possession")—and that is with the God of nothing less than the "whole earth." There is surely emphasized here a real sense of the aspect of privilege that is Israel's. Further, within this relationship Israel is to be a "priestly kingdom," and we may question what is meant by this expression. It is highly unlikely that the writer, or writers, had in mind here that all the members of the nation would become priests serving at the sacrificial altars and attending to further priestly duties, especially in the religious instruction of their peoples. It would seem rather that we should understand it as expressing something of a spiritual nature; that is, as the priests of the line of Aaron would approach the Lord on behalf of their people and offer their sacrifices, so too do the people of Israel have a privileged place of closeness to, and fellowship with the Lord. That is, they are in a particular and special "spiritual" relationship with the Lord; in fact they are a "holy" people, that is, a people who are set apart in their special relationship with God. One writer has said by way of comment on this, "The image presented is that of the unique and exclusive possession, and that image is expanded by what appears to be an addition ('for to me belongs the whole earth') to suggest the 'crown jewel' of a large collection, the masterwork, the one-of-a-kind piece." Yet there are laid down by God upon these people who thus come into covenant relationship with him, these Ten Commandments, this Decalogue set out in Exod 20:1–17, in this version depicted as words which God spoke. They are also set out in Deut 5:6–21, in that account as the words of Moses who is recounting what God revealed to him on Mount Horeb (which seems to be the same mountain as Sinai in the Exodus account).

Exodus 20:2 and Deut 5:2, 6, and 7 express the fundamental role of the Lord in this covenant; he was the one who brought his people out of Egypt and slavery; and the people of Israel are to have no other gods besides him. Deut 5:3 makes the point that the Israelites as they read and ponder the commandments should not think of them as merely historical, coming from times earlier than their contemporary settings, but rather indeed as utterly contemporary—"Not with our ancestors did the LORD make this covenant, but with us, who are all of us here alive today." The author, or authors, of Deuteronomy are anxious that any generation—and indeed, all generations—of contemporary readers of the Ten Commandments should feel that it is with *them* that the Lord is making the covenant. Further, in addition to being reminded about who the Lord of this covenant relationship is, the people are commanded not to have anything to do with idols, and it is stressed that they are to have nothing to do with any possible, conceivable idols, whether they be on the earth, above the earth, or under the earth. There is emphasis here on the severest judgment being upon all those who have anything to do with such idols. Yet also there will be with them, these faithful worshippers of the Lord, the steadfast love of this same Lord throughout the future generations (Exod 20:4–6; Deut 5:8–10).

Then follow commandments that the people are not to make wrongful use of the name of the Lord (Exod 20:7; Deut 5:11), perhaps meaning that the Lord's name is to be honored and respected, to be praised and blessed, and certainly not to be either dishonored or disrespected. The next commandment seems to have been particularly important in the estimation of those who compiled these documents, for it is set out in very considerable detail, even we may say, elaborately; it is the command concerning the honoring of the Sabbath day, in particular that it is to be a day of rest for *all* people, not least for those who are servants, or even slaves (Exod 20:8–11; Deut 5:12–15). This commandment is about people living with respect for other members of their community, and especially those with little power or authority. Prophets such as Amos (see Amos 8:4–8) castigated the wealthy who did not wish those working for them to experience and benefit from this day of rest. Other parts of the Old Testament also place particular emphasis on this matter, and in the course of this study we shall return to it.

This elaborately explained commandment is followed by a series of further commandments that are more briefly stated: in fact after the one about honoring parents in Exod 20:12 and Deut 5:16, the remainder are without explanatory comments. Yet there is to be no murder, no adultery, no stealing, no bearing false witness, though the final one does have some explanatory fleshing out, concerning not coveting anything that belongs to one's neighbors (Exod 20:13–17; Deut 5:16–21).

We see here that our writers have added to their accounts of the Lord's deliverance of his people from their hardships and sufferings in Egypt these succinct statements of his expectations of them as their lives progressed and developed. There is little doubt that the writers here were in fact situated in the land of promise where in spite of problems there were also manifold temptations to forget both their earlier deliverances and now their new neighbors around them. They were faced with the temptation to live for themselves alone. Here they are reminded of humanity's ever-present need of divine deliverances, and at the same time of the never-ending need of a community's care for both its members and its neighbors.

This covenant is spoken of in Exodus 24 as having been concluded and solemnized, parts of this being done on earth at the foot of mount Sinai and parts up the mountain, where Moses and Aaron, Nadab and Abihu, along with seventy of the elders of Israel went, on behalf of the people where we are told, they actually *saw* the Lord (24:10–11). The fact that these men actually *saw* God is surely significant, for the Old Testament does not always in such situations portray human being as actually *seeing* God—certainly not seeing God and still living (see for example Exod 33:20; and even more extreme Job 23:15). But here surely, what we have is a remarkable theological attempt to set down in words something of the wonder that a human being must feel in the very presence of the Lord. Thus we read,

> . . . and they saw the God of Israel. Under his feet there was something like a pavement of sapphire stone, like the very heaven for clearness. God did not lay his hand on the chief men of the people of Israel; also they beheld God, and they ate and drank. (Exod 24:10–11)

Yet the account continues, if anything emphasizing the more the great-ness of the Lord, and the remarkable experience for any human of being so near to the divine presence:

> Then Moses went up on the mountain, and the cloud covered the mountain. The glory of the LORD settled on Mount Sinai, and the cloud covered it for six days; on the seventh day he called to Moses out of the cloud. Now the appearance of the glory of the LORD was like a devouring fire on the top of the mountain in the sight of the people of Israel. Moses entered the cloud, and went up on the mountain. Moses was on the mountain for forty days and forty nights. (Exod 24:15–18)

There then follows what is portrayed as a series of detailed instructions from the Lord to Moses about the people making offers of gifts which will be used in the building of a place of worship and the furnishing thereof with suitable religious artefacts. See Exodus 25:1—31:18. That is, the people having experienced the delivering might of the Lord applied on their behalf, then Moses and the leaders and elders of the people having been on the holy mountain experiencing the glory and the greatness of the Lord, are now be-ing called upon to establish either a place, or else a number of places, where the people can seek God and offer their worship.

Yet what seems strange is that these commands and instructions are presented as those that are to be carried out and effected there in the desert, and—even further—by a people who were in the midst of escaping from their previous lives in Egypt, people who are portrayed as having little more than the clothes on their backs and the shoes on their feet. And where would all the gold and silver, and other precious metals and other objects be found in the desert areas in such quantities as are spoken about here (see Exod 25:3, 11–13, 17–18 and so on; see further Exod 26:19, 21, 25, 32 and so on)?

What, however, is much more understandable as a place for the seek-ing of and worshipping the Lord in the desert setting in which the pilgrim people found themselves, is the tent, the Tent of Meeting. We are told that Moses made this, and here he met God face to face, and when he did so there was a pillar of cloud at the entrance, towards which the people would bow down as they stood at the entrances of their own tents, for in that Tent of Meeting, "the LORD used to speak to Moses face to face, as one speaks to a friend. Then he would return to the camp; but his young assistant, Joshua son of Nun, would not leave the tent." (Exod 33:11) That sounds like a suit-able, appropriate and understandable sanctuary for the desert setting. But what are we to say about what is called both "sanctuary" and also "taber-nacle"? Within this was the Ark of the Covenant (whose carrying poles were of acacia wood overlaid with gold), and also the "mercy-seat," a table of acacia wood overlaid with pure gold, and lampstands of gold. This surely sounds remarkably like the temple that came to be built in Jerusalem in the days of King Solomon, suggesting that it was a retrojected portrayal of that temple of Solomon *back* into the desert days and setting. Yet perhaps what is crucial about this portrayal as having been built in the desert—but which in fact seems much more likely to have been built years later in Jerusalem—is that it was set forth as what was commanded by God on the mount, the mountain, Sinai/Horeb. For had it not been shown to Moses "on the mountain" (Exod 25:40; 26:30; 27:8)?

Yet what has been set forth in these extensive chapters, coming as they do after the account of the Israelites' deliverance from Egypt under the Pharaoh who "did not know Joseph" (Exod 1:8), is a vital part of the whole covenant-making procedure about the Israelites' future life, a life founded on their trust in the delivering Lord, and having the commitment on their part to be faithful to him, to worship him, and him alone—having no other gods and no idols (Exod 20:2–6). Rather, they must worship the Lord God, and him alone, and here as a vital part of this holy, covenantal relationship are the instructions about the sanctuary that is to be at the heart of their worship, the setting for their worship, and that in its grandeur—not forgetting its various divinely-specified furnishings and appurtenances—is to be the very meeting point of the Lord and his people, and also for the people the great symbol and physical representation of their faith. It is surely understandable that such instructions about the sanctuary for the worship of, and the meeting with, their Lord should be set forth as a vital part of this whole great body of theology about covenant and deliverance, about human dependence on, and commitment to, this God of the exodus, the desert, and the holy mountain.

However, the book of Exodus has more that calls for consideration—and more also that is germane to our particular study. For we read in Exod 25:1—31:18 that Moses spent a period of time up the mountain receiving instructions for the building of the above-mentioned sanctuary, but that meanwhile on the earth below there was a commotion in the Israelite camp (32:1—33:23). The Israelites, in the absence of Moses complained that nothing was happening, and prevailed upon Aaron to make gods for them who would lead them out of the desert. Clearly, they were being tempted to commit the sin of believing that God would not carry out his promise to be with them forever, so they manufactured a god, cast in gold in the form of a bull image, and, "They rose early the next day, and offered burnt offerings and brought sacrifices of well-being; and the people sat down to eat and drink, and rose up to revel." (Exod 32:6)

Meanwhile, Moses—still on the mountain—was informed, we are told, by the Lord about what was happening on earth, and in response Moses implored God to forgive the people (32:11–13), as a result of which "And the LORD changed his mind about the disaster that he planned to bring on his people." (32:14) Even so, we read that the Lord was resolved to bring his judgment upon the people, which resulted in Moses once again appealing to the Lord for the divine mercies, Moses perhaps even offering his own life— the text in its brevity is not at all clear at this point—interceding desperately with the Lord, "Alas, this people has sinned a great sin; they have made for themselves gods of gold. But now, if you will only forgive their sin—but if not, blot me out of the book that you have written." (Exod 32:31)

Then in Exodus 33, where we hear about various matters following on from the incident of the golden calf, we read of the construction and use of the tent we have already considered, and about Moses only partially "seeing" the Lord on the mountain, only seeing his back, not his face (33:12–23). This is followed in Exodus 34 with the renewal of the earlier covenant which had been broken through the people's sin of not trusting in the leadership of the Lord, and the first occurrence of something in the nature of a liturgical formula that will in varying words and forms appear in other books of the Old Testament:

> The LORD, the LORD,
> a God merciful and gracious,
> slow to anger,
> and abounding in steadfast love and faithfulness,
> keeping steadfast love for the thousandth generation,
> forgiving iniquity and transgression and sin,
> yet by no means clearing the guilty,
> but visiting the iniquity of the parents upon the children
> and the children's children
> to the third and the fourth generation. (Exod 34:6–7. See also
> Pss 86:15; 103:8; 145:8; Num 14:18; Joel 2:13; Nah 1:3; Neh
> 9:17; Jonah 4:2)

Also in Exodus 34 is another arrangement of the earlier Ten Commandments, this time with a more liturgical, ritual emphasis, which has therefore been called the "Ritual Decalogue," and includes instructions to observe a number of annual feasts and festivals (34:10–28). The chapter ends with Moses coming down the mountain, now with a new set of the tablets of the covenant, and with his shining face (34:29–35). And with that the book of Exodus has one final part, which on first reading may seem to be tediously repetitive of what earlier Moses had been instructed to make by way of sanctuary. While previously we read about the instructions as to what the Israelites under the leadership of Moses were to build as a great sanctuary, now here in Exod 35:1—40:38 we read about the actual construction of the same. But this great sanctuary that came to be built in Jerusalem, along with other aspects of the general subject of the worship of the Lord God, will make up the main content of ch 3 of this present work.

From Texts to Spirituality

What do the Old Testament passages that we have considered in this chapter contribute to a Christian spirituality in the present-day world? What is there in the texts we have considered that is *not* present in the New Testament, and therefore for their particular emphases and insights we are dependent upon the Old Testament?

In the first place we should speak of the subject that dominates the beginning of the Old Testament, namely the creation of the heavens and the earth, and we should surely recall the sense of awe and wonder that infuses these chapters of Genesis concerning the wisdom, power and greatness of the Lord God. Further, a vital part of these accounts of creation is the culminating creation of the human beings in such ways that they are privileged to have, and can be expected to have, fellowship and harmony in their lives with the Creator, and moreover to act in ways that will fulfill the Lord's purposes in his good creation. Further, the human beings have a distinctive and very special place in the creation in that they have been made in this special way. They are portrayed as having a quite special, distinctive, indeed *spiritual*, relationship with the Lord for they have been made in the *image*, in the *likeness* of the Lord. Thus there is a real sense in these early chapters in the book of Genesis of the element of awe and wonder, in no small way concerning what the Lord has willed and effected. Of this great God Job in one of his speeches proclaimed, in what is surely a real sense of awesome wonder at the work of the Creator, and what a wondrous being this Lord must be:

> By his power he stilled the Sea;
> by his understanding he struck down Rahab.
> By his wind the heavens were made fair;
> his hand pierced the fleeing serpent.
> These are indeed but the outskirts of his ways;
> and how small a whisper do we hear of him!
> But the thunder of his power who can understand? (Job 26:12–14)

This surely has a word, a message for us, a yet most-relevant and appropriate word for us about this aspect of awe and wonder in our worship of God, and in our living out the life of the gospel in the world of today. The Word may in the fullness of time have become flesh for us, but that in itself should surely engender within us a sense of added, renewed awesome wonder about the mysterious workings of the on-going providential care of the Lord. We are surely once again being reminded of the words of awe expressed in the account of Isaiah's vision of the Lord in the Jerusalem temple, his decisive encounter with the holy One:

> In the year that King Uzziah died, I saw the Lord sitting on a throne, high and lofty; and the hem of his robe filled the temple. Seraphs were in attendance above him; each had six wings: with two they covered their faces, and with two they covered their feet, and with two they flew. And one called to another and said:
> "Holy, holy, holy is the Lord of hosts;
> the whole earth is full of his glory." (Isa 6:1–3)

Yet the further wonder is that the Lord should choose human beings to have a particular life of fellowship with him, those who will live under his guidance, who will experience his will and power to deliver his people from troubles great and small, and who will be called to live for him, and to live lives of service in obedience to his will. As we have seen, the word that is given to this divine-human relationship in the Old Testament is "covenant," a word that occurs in so many of the Old Testament's books. Still, this concern of God is not just for his particular people, Abraham and his descendants, but in fact for all people, as is movingly made clear in the Genesis story of the flood with Noah and the ark, and as we shall come to see, elsewhere. Yet in the midst of these stories of God's creating and caring activities, there is the reality of human sinfulness, and that ever-present temptation to neglect the ways of the Lord, for his people to fail in their trusting the Lord, and even to make their own gods. Surely, how realistic and down-to-earth are these writers and theologians of ancient Israel! Thus in Genesis 4:7 we have the divine warning being solemnly given to Cain, "sin is lurking at the door; its desire is for you . . . ." Yet as the unknown author of *The Cloud of Unknowing* wrote,

> Every day original sin will produce new, fresh sinful impulses, and every day you must smite them down, and hasten to shear them off with the sharp two-edged sword of discretion. In ways like this we learn that there is no real security or true rest in this life!

Yet the purposes of God are portrayed in these opening parts of the Old Testament as continuing, and in later books we may read about divine provisions for human sins to be forgiven. Already we have observed how in the book of Exodus there is affirmed in a remarkable way the powerful presence of the Lord for the saving and deliverance of the people, and how these accounts lead into covenant making, and remaking, and also in a major way into the provision of worthy places for worship. No doubt what is portrayed as having been given "on the mountain" to Moses and those close to him, was intended to apply in a special way to what was in the fullness of time established in Jerusalem. But it may be said that such matters are also to be taken with great seriousness in all ages of the ongoing lives of both the Israelite and the Christian communities. In this way they are spoken of by the writer of the Letter to the Hebrews, for example in Heb 9:18–21 (but also elsewhere in this "letter"), in his presentation of Christ as the mediator of the new covenant. See also Heb 8:6, 8, 9, 10; 9:4; 10:16, 29; 12:24; 13:20. Further, it is surely not without significance that the first chapter of the gospel according to Luke—a chapter that must be intended to provide a real link-up and to establish a relationship and a connection with all that happened under the Lord in the past and is recorded in the Old Testament, and what will happen in Christ and is recorded in the New Testament—does indeed use the word and language of "covenant." This we find in the so-called Song of Zechariah (Luke 1:67–79), where it is said of the new savior who is soon to be born,

> Thus he has shown the mercy promised to our ancestors,
>   and has remembered his holy *covenant*,
> the oath that he swore to our ancestor Abraham,
>   to grant us that we, being rescued from the hands of our enemies,
> might serve him without fear, in holiness and righteousness
>   before him all our days. (Luke 1:72–74)

Nor should we forget the ongoing use of, and significance of, the Ten Commandments for later generations of worshippers and seekers. How very many worshippers of both Jewish and Christian faiths will over the years have seen those words inscribed upon the Church, Chapel, Meeting House or Cathedral walls, so that perhaps as for Martin Luther those commandments were to do with nothing less than a total transformation, a change of thought, word and deed, in turning from doing any possible harm to one's neighbor but rather to treating them with patience, love, and kindness. Luther said that it was only as one entrusted oneself to, and continued to cling to him that we can live as the commandments direct us. Thus, surely

in these various ways do we see something of the ongoing significance of
the Old Testament for the life of Christian spirituality. And further, in these
biblical accounts of the creation of the world and those of the ongoing relationships between the Lord and his works of creation and with the peoples,
there is something that resonates for us in those famous spiritual thoughts
of Julian of Norwich concerning that small object in the palm of the hand,
the size of a hazel-nut, about which various questions were asked which
resulted in deep assurance:

> "It lasts and will last for ever because God loves it; and in the
> same way everything exists through the love of God." In this
> little thing I saw three attributes: the first is that God made it,
> the second is that he loves it, the third is that God cares for it.
> But what does that mean to me? Truly, the maker, the lover, the
> carer; for until I become one substance with him, I can never
> have love, rest or true bliss; that is to say, until I am so bound to
> him that there may be no created thing between my God and
> me.

Indeed, as also Saint Augustine expressed the matter at the very beginning of his *Confessions*, saying that the thought of God stirs the humans,
"because you made us for yourself and our hearts find no peace until they
rest in you."

But there are many other matters in which the Old Testament scriptures contribute to our Christian spirituality which we will be considering
in the chapters that now follow.

2

Life with Deliverance and Judgment

> How can I give you up, Ephraim?
>> How can I hand you over, O Israel?
> How can I make you like Admah?
>> How can I treat you like Zeboiim?
> My heart recoils within me;
>> my compassion grows warm and tender.
> I will not execute my fierce anger;
>> I will not again destroy Ephraim;
> for I am God and no mortal,
>> the Holy One in your midst,
>> and I will not come in wrath. (Hos 11:8–9)

HOSEA CHAPTER 11, VERSES 1–9 is one of the most moving passages in the whole of the Old Testament, for the prophet here is imagining what must be going on in the innermost being of the Lord, for he, the Lord, has been witness to the exceeding sinfulness of his people Israel, to their continual backsliding from his divine plans and purposes for them. Instead of worshipping the Lord God, and serving him alone, they have worshipped the Canaanite deities, and offered incense to idols (Hos 11:2), with the result that the first reaction of the Lord God is portrayed as being one of dreadful judgment upon the people. But then—and this is expressed in deeply powerful and heart-felt language, the language of a loving earthly father's mature reactions to the sins of his much loved but at the same time considerably wayward child—something happens deep within the heart of God, and his compassion grows warm and tender (v. 8), so that in fact the Lord cannot bring himself to effect his judgment upon those he loves so profoundly and dearly. Thus does the prophet Hosea most movingly portray something of a tussle that there must be in the heart of God, as God is, so to speak, torn between his judgment upon his people's sinfulness on the one hand, and on the other with his overwhelming love for them.

It is commonly asserted that the Old Testament has too much in it about the judgment of God, that although there may be other emphases as well, its usefulness in the life of the Christian Church and in the study and thinking of individual Christians is thereby limited, some Christians might say, severely limited. However, it has to be said that the Old Testament has within it from beginning to end the burning conviction that God is the holy and righteous Lord, and merely to be in his near presence carries with it an overwhelming sense of concern on the part of the human person involved, such a one being even the more convicted of his or her sinfulness. Thus the reaction of the prophet-to-be Isaiah when he is confronted by the Lord is, "Woe is me! I am lost, for I am a man of unclean lips, and I live among a people of unclean lips; yet my eyes have seen the King, the LORD of hosts!" (Isa 6:5) has become something of a classic reaction also for so many of those who find themselves in the presence of this same God, and also those who seek to be faithful followers of him in their lives on earth.

Nevertheless there may be Christians who find it is difficult to believe all those many parts of the Old Testament where it is asserted that this and that incidence of suffering of an individual or a group is due to their having sinned. Clearly there are situations in life where individual people suffer for inexplicable reasons, and these are matters we shall turn to in ch 6 of this work. In the meantime, however, we may take note of the fact that when the man Job finds himself confronted with the holy God he is hard pressed to be able to say anything. Further, perhaps one of the most vital aspects of the book of Job would seem to be the proclamation of the sheer surpassing greatness and almightiness, the holiness and mystery, that is the Lord whose ways and deeds cannot at all times be understood. But to this we shall return.

This, however, is not to say that the Old Testament does not have a deep and firm belief in the holiness of the Lord, and that all too often there is the spirit of divine judgment upon those sinful humans who look to the Lord for his guidance, help and direction in their lives. Above all there is the conviction of many a human person that they are sinners who ever must come to the appointed places of worship and seek the divine forgiveness. For there in those appointed places are the regularly enacted rites of the Israelite cult specifically dedicated to the purposes of securing forgiveness of sins, either through sacrifices and offerings, or through prayer, the latter either by the sinner himself or herself, or by another, or even others. The prophet Hosea is portrayed as giving to his people, who fully aware of their sins, a prayer with which they may seek to approach the Lord. Thus they are to say to the Lord,

> Take away all guilt;
> accept that which is good,
>   and we will offer
>   the fruit of our lips.
> Assyria shall not save us;
>   we will not ride upon horses;
> we will say no more, "Our God,"
>   to the work of our hands.
> In you the orphan finds mercy. (Hos 14:2b–3)

Here the worshippers confess themselves totally dependent on the Lord and his great mercy. In fact, it is as if this person would be totally lost were it not for this overwhelming and forgiving love of God.

Or we may consider Ps 130, which near its beginning gives eloquent expression to the psalmist's awareness, his deep and troubling conviction of his sinfulness ("If you, O LORD, should mark iniquities, LORD, who could stand?" [Ps 130:3]).

Nevertheless, by the end of the composition there is a profound expression of confidence in the Lord's love, and in both his will and his power to forgive his people all their iniquities. Thus,

> O Israel, hope in the LORD!
> For with the LORD there is steadfast love,
>   and with him is great power to redeem.
> It is he who will redeem Israel
>   from all its iniquities. (Ps 130:7–8)

Further, there are a large number of psalms in the Psalter that speak of the sufferings and problems of an individual person, presumably either of a psalmist or someone else, and where the earlier part of the composition is taken up with all the things that are going badly for this individual. In Ps 5 we read of the psalmist's sighing (v. 1), yet of his confidence that the Lord does hear his prayer (v. 3), for indeed he is a God of abundant steadfast love (vv. 4–7), so that by the end there is the expression of sure faith that the Lord's devotees will ever sing his praises, for indeed he does cover the righteous with his favor "as with a shield",

> But let all who take refuge in you rejoice;
>   let them ever sing for joy.
> Spread your protection over them,

> so that those who love your name may exult in you.
> For you bless the righteous, O Lord;
>   you cover them with favor as with a shield. (Ps 5:11–12)

It has to be said that this theme of the Lord's deliverance of his people is indeed a strong and predominant one in the Old Testament. Further, the theme is indeed well represented in the book of Psalms, where we have a very considerable number of psalms in which an individual laments their present very troubled situation. These have, unsurprisingly, been called Individual Lament Psalms, and they appear in particular in the earlier parts of the Psalter.

Both of Psalms 6 and 7 are examples of these. We note how in Ps 6 the psalmist is asking the Lord to be gracious to him, for not only is he "languishing" but also his "bones are shaking with terror" (v. 2).

It reads as if the psalmist is ill, or that he is confronted with truly scary possibilities in his life. In some of the verses that follow it would seem to be the former, for in v. 5 we have talk of death, and there is rehearsed that predominant belief expressed in so much of the Old Testament that after death there is "no remembrance" of the Lord, and that in Sheol—that place to which in the thought of the Old Testament those who have died go—there is no possibility of praising God. But in other verses we read of the psalmist's foes (v. 7), "workers of evil" (v. 8), and at the same time we read of the psalmist's confidence that the Lord has heard his cry, accepting his prayer (vv. 8–9), and that thus this suffering one is much more hopeful, becoming sure that his enemies will come to be ashamed, indeed struck with terror and turned back (v. 10). The following psalm, Ps 7, displays very much the same type of structure, presumably reflecting an individual psalmist's experiences. This psalm has a somewhat lengthy recital of the problems that this person is experiencing (Ps 7:1–16), but it ends with a most confident expression of thanksgiving to the Lord, and with the singing of praise to the name of the Lord, the Most High (v. 17).

Another of these psalms of Individual Lament is Psalm 3, in which we are hearing a psalmist crying out to God, and speaking of his considerable distress. Thus we read,

> O Lord, how many are my foes!
>   Many are rising against me;
> many are saying to me,
>   "There is no help for you in God." (Ps 3:1–2)

Yet later in this psalm we read about a remarkable change of mood:

> I lie down and sleep;

> I wake again, for the LORD sustains me.
> I am not afraid of tens of thousands of people
> who have set themselves against me all around.
>
> . . . . .
>
> Deliverance belongs to the LORD;
> may your blessing be on your people! (Ps 3:5–6, 8)

There, surely, in the words of v. 8 is nothing less than the psalmist making a confession of faith, "Deliverance belongs to the LORD", that is, there is help available for a person in God, help that may not otherwise be found. This, what we may surely call an expression of faith, is also to be found in slightly different wording expressed in Prov 21:31.

As well as these psalms that speak of individuals making their laments to the Lord out of their various experiences of suffering, there is also a smaller number of psalms that have been called communal laments. In these the whole nation appears to be crying out to God in the face of the sufferings that many, even perhaps all, are experiencing. Thus, for example, there is Ps 79 which speaks of the nations having come to Jerusalem where they have defiled the temple and laid the city in ruins (Ps 79:1). Even so, here again is the expression of hope by the close of the psalm, with the psalmist saying that the people will at some unspecified future time once more give thanks to God, and that thus from generation to generation his praises will indeed be recounted (Ps 79:13).

Another of these so-called Communal Lament psalms with a confident ending is Ps 85, in which we again seem to be hearing about the sufferings of the whole community, even perhaps the whole nation which finds itself in a setting of great difficulty. Here is again a psalmist who appears to be the speaking one, and who is endeavoring to give expression to the distress of the whole people. In this way:

> Restore us again, O God of our salvation,
> and put away your indignation toward us.
> Will you be angry with us forever?
> Will you prolong your anger to all generations?
>
> . . . . .
>
> Steadfast love and faithfulness will meet;
> righteousness and peace will kiss each other.
> Faithfulness will spring up from the ground,
> and righteousness will look down from the sky.
> The LORD will give what is good,
> and our land will yield its increase.
> Righteousness will go before him,
> and will make a path for his steps. (Ps 85:4–5, 10–13)

Thus does a whole community, even perhaps the whole nation, feel the confidence of the divine deliverance, and there is surely expressed in this psalm a renewed sense of trust in both the will and also the power of the Lord to deliver these people.

What we are encountering here is the theme of the delivering mercies and strength of the Lord. It is acknowledged that in the world things will at times be exceedingly difficult for God's people, both as individuals and also as a corporate body, but that with God there is more often than not the experience of deliverance—or at least the confidence that there will one day be that deliverance. This we have observed in many of the psalms both of individual lament, and also of communal lament.

We continue, then, with the theme of God's deliverance of his peoples from their present troublesome experiences. In the Old Testament the most dramatic and far reaching example of this divine deliverance of God's people is the whole story of the rescue of the people of Israel from their corporate life in Egypt in the days when they were groaning under the harsh conditions of slavery. In these days, we are told, the people cried out to the Lord, and moreover that "God heard their groaning, and God remembered his covenant with Abraham, Isaac, and Jacob. God looked upon the Israelites, and God took notice of them." (Exod 2:24–25) This is followed by the appearance of the Lord to Moses on the mountain called Horeb—or in other parts of the Old Testament Sinai—where God speaks to and calls Moses to be involved in the divine deliverance. First comes the word about what God will do,

> "I am the God of your father, the God of Abraham, the God of Isaac, and the God of Jacob." And Moses hid his face, for he was afraid to look at God.
>
> Then the LORD said, "I have observed the misery of my people who are in Egypt; I have heard their cry on account of their taskmasters. Indeed, I know their sufferings, and I have come down to deliver them from the Egyptians, and to bring them up out of that land to a good and broad land, a land flowing with milk and honey, to the country of the Canaanities, the Hittites, the Amorites, the Perizzites, the Hivites, and the Jebusites. The cry of Israelites has now come to me; I have also seen how the Egyptians oppress them." (Exod 3:6–9)

From a later historical situation we have the Lord's promise to his people of Judah and Jerusalem that in the face of the siege of Jerusalem by the Assyrians the Lord would deliver his people once again (2 Kings 20:6). That particular deliverance would last for a limited historical time, for in the days of the Babylonians—the world power coming in succession to the Assyrians—Jerusalem would be defeated, the temple and much else by way of buildings being razed to the ground, and many of its people, including in particular many of their leaders, being taken away into Babylon where they would remain for around half a century as exiles in a foreign land.

Yet some fifty or so years later Persians under their leader Cyrus took control of Babylon, and allowed those who were exiles from their own countries to return to their lands and resume their earlier lives there, on the conditions that they paid their taxes to the Persians and prayed for their Persian overlord. Thus did the Persians have a very different policy regarding its subject peoples than did the earlier Assyrian and Babylonian rulers. For the prophet of Isaiah chs 40–55 this was interpreted as the fulfillment of the will of the Lord God of Israel to bring his people back to their homeland, their promised land, and it was thus understood as a deliverance on the part of the Lord for his people, once more in captivity. In fact, in the thrilling words of the prophet of Isa 40–55, this was understood to be a new Exodus, like that earlier one from Egypt, but this time from Babylon. Further, whereas that earlier exodus had of necessity to be undertaken quietly, surreptitiously, an exit effected in the night time, this time rather in some triumph, imagined as being on raised-up roads, as if over leveled hills (Isa 40:3–4), and portrayed as in full view of all the nations— "Then the glory of the LORD shall be revealed, and all people shall see it together, for the mouth of the LORD has spoken." (Isa 40:5)

This exodus from Babylon, this deliverance from captivity, is portrayed in its greatness as being something so thrilling and new; thus for example this time, so unlike it had been experienced in the first Exodus, there will be no thirsting in the wilderness. Thus,

> Do not remember the former things,
> or consider the things of old.
> I am about to do a new thing;
> now it springs forth, do you not perceive it?
> I will make a way in the wilderness
> and rivers in the desert.
> The wild animals will honor me,
> the jackals and the ostriches;
> for I give water in the wilderness,
> rivers in the desert,
> to give drink to my chosen people,
> the people whom I formed for myself
> so that they might declare my praise. (Isa 43:18–21)

These thrilling chapters in the Isaiah book are brought to glorious climax in the words which close this part of that book:

> For you shall go out in joy,
>   and be led back in peace;
> the mountains and the hills before you
>   shall burst into song,
>   and all the trees of the field shall clap their hands.
> Instead of the thorn shall come up the cypress;
>   instead of the brier shall come up the myrtle;
> and it shall be to the LORD for a memorial,
>   for an everlasting sign that shall not be cut off. (Isa 55:12–13)

Deliverance is a major theme in the Old Testament, and those significant deliverances in life are portrayed as being works of the Lord. There may be human intermediaries, such as a Moses, or a Persian King Cyrus, yet even so these human characters are depicted as acting under the presiding will and guiding hand of the Lord God. The words "deliver" and "deliverance" appear with remarkable frequency in the books of the Old Testament, as can readily be witnessed by consulting a biblical concordance. Yet it also needs to be said that this theme of deliverance is but a part of that overarching biblical concept of covenant which we have considered in the first chapter of this work. That is, the affirmation that the Lord has graciously called his chosen people Israel into a relationship with himself, that he for his part will keep, guide and protect his people, while they for theirs are called to worship and serve him alone, living in obedience to his commands and wishes.

We should perhaps pause at this stage of our consideration of some of the contributions in the Old Testament on the subject of God's deliverance of his people. While it may be the case in the last example we have chosen—that of Cyrus, king of the Persians—of a number of exiles of different peoples and nationalities being allowed to go home to their own lands, in those earlier stories of the deliverance of the people of Israel it seems to be of the people of Israel alone. So what are we to say about those other peoples who feature in the later events of Israel's deliverance? And what about the attitudes portrayed in the Old Testament towards other peoples? What are we going to think and say about that passage in Deut 7, which sets out what at least some Old Testament writers felt about the Lord's relationships with on the one hand the people of Israel and on the other with some other peoples. Thus we read:

> When the LORD your God brings you into the land that you
> are about to enter and occupy, and he clears away many nations
> before you—the Hittites, the Girgashites, the Amorites, the

Canaanites, the Perizzites, the Hivites, and the Jebusites, seven
nations mightier and more numerous than you—and when the
LORD your God gives them over to you and you defeat them,
then you must utterly destroy them. Make no covenant with
them and show them no mercy. Do not intermarry with them,
giving your daughters to their sons or taking their daughters for
your sons . . . (Deut 7:1–3)

Now the word used in the above quotation about the people of Israel
being ordered to "utterly destroy" those seven other nations is surely very
difficult for Christians to read. Not only are the words "utterly destroy" expressed grammatically in strong words, but so also is the thought behind
them. As one scholar in a recent detailed study has said,

One moment we see God as loving; the next moment we see a
deity who apparently sponsors mass murder. How should this
be approached and understood?

Not surprisingly, a range of suggestions have been put forward to deal
with this difficulty, for example, that a ban has been put on any dealings
with these other nations, or that it should be understood as a most serious
demand for the people of Israel to give unqualified allegiance to the Lord
and his commands concerning the purity of the Israelite people and nation.
Although these suggestions may possibly give us some sense of direction
and guidance about these words, they surely still leave us with a very great
problem, such is their exceedingly harsh tone about the peoples of other
nations and how they should be treated. Indeed, we perhaps have to say that
these are some of the teachings of the Old Testament that are regarded by
many as inappropriate for use in our lives of attempted Christian spirituality.

There is another aspect to this theme of the Lord's deliverance of his
people, namely their continued need of the Lord's help and guidance in
what may be new conditions for them, or even in a new land. Thus, for
example, when that son of Adam and Eve, Cain had killed his brother Abel,
and therefore had to flee to a new land, we are told,

And the LORD put a mark on Cain, so that no one who came
upon him would kill him. Then Cain went away from the presence of the LORD, and settled in the land of Nod, east of Eden.
(Gen 4:15–16)

So even sinful fugitive Cain was granted divine help and protection.

Or we may consider the plight of the Israelite escapees from Egypt
under the leadership of Moses, and we are hardly surprised to read that having been delivered from the power of the Pharaoh (Exod 12–13) and having

safely crossed the sea (Exod 14), they are portrayed as singing the praises of the Lord is exalted tones (Exod 15). But then what was there to eat and drink in the desert, in that wilderness which, we are told, was,

> the wilderness of Sin, which is between Elim and Sinai, on the fifteenth day of the second month after they had departed from the land of Egypt. The whole congregation of the Israelites complained against Moses and Aaron in the wilderness. The Israelites said to them, "If only we had died by the hand of the LORD in the land of Egypt, when we sat by the fleshpots and ate our fill of bread; for you have brought us out into this wilderness to kill this whole assembly with hunger." (Exod 16:1–3)

Thus were there given to the Israelites in the desert the gifts of food (Exod 16:4–36) and drink (Exod 17:1–7). Moreover, there would be much more portrayed as what was to come, nothing less than the covenant constitution for the whole of their future existence as the people of God, with the assurance of God's continued guidance of them. Further, there would be details of the provision of places where God could be heard, spoken to, and worshipped, along with what are surely instructions and plans for those days, far into the future, in the promised land, all this being recorded for us in the extended narrative in Exodus 19:1—40:38. Yet this material is surely to make the salient point that these are together nothing less than the gracious provisions of God for his people in one particular age, but which are also symbolic and illustrative of the provision that the Lord makes for his people in age after age. Indeed, as we read in the New Testament, in John's Gospel:

> Our ancestors ate the manna in the wilderness; as it is written, "He gave them bread from heaven to eat." Then Jesus said to them, "Very truly, I tell you, it was not Moses who gave you the bread from heaven, but it is my Father who gives you the true bread from heaven. For the bread of God is that which comes down from heaven and gives life to the world." (John 6:31–33)

While in this covenant relationship there are the Lord's many and varied acts of deliverance of his people, yet we should also take notice of the fact that there are also the Lord's judgments on the failings and sins of his people. Nevertheless, as we have already observed, and shall come to see in a later chapter in more detail, not all setbacks of the Lord's people can be, or should be, explained as divine judgments upon them. There are in worldly life those setbacks and tragedies that cannot reasonably be attributed to human sinfulness, and are in fact in human terms inexplicable. We shall return to this later (see ch 6 below), but for the present we should take note of the fact that in the divine covenant relationship as well as there being the deliverances, there are also the judgments of the Lord upon his people for their sinful ways and actions. There are, for example, in Leviticus 26 and Deuteronomy 28 lists of warnings for God's people, a setting out of a whole series of acts and ways of life that are unacceptable to the Lord of the covenant, the committing of which will bring upon them the divine judgment.

So, for example, in the prophecy of Amos we have a series of passages about the transgressions of various of the nations surrounding Judah and Israel (Amos 1:3—2:3), and also of Judah and Israel. The prophet's condemnation of Judah is because the people have rejected the law of the Lord, not keeping his statutes. That is, they have failed to do what the Lord has commanded them to do.

> Thus says the LORD:
> For three transgressions of Judah,
>   and for four, I will not revoke the punishment;
> because they have rejected the law of the LORD,
>   and have not kept his statutes,
> but they have been led astray by the same lies
>   after which their ancestors walked. (Amos 2:4)

And then Amos turns to his own people, that is the people of Israel, and he has more to say to them than he is recorded as saying about the people of Judah. (Israel and Judah being those two kingdoms into which the previously united tribes became divided after the death of King Solomon.) What is of particular interest and significance here is that a central complaint of the prophet Amos about his people concerns the ways in which they are living with their neighbors. His complaints in fact are to do with the lack of social righteousness, rather than about matters of correctness in their sanctuary worship of the Lord. In the Amos passage that now follows, the sole reference to sanctuary worship is the complaint about the comforting use of blankets that appear to have been taken as pledges against debts of money, and drinking wines purchased with ill-gotten gains:

> Thus says the LORD:
> For three transgressions of Israel,
>   and for four, I will not revoke the punishment;
> because they sell the righteous for silver,
>   and the needy for a pair of sandals—
> they who trample the head of the poor into the dust of the earth,
>   and push the afflicted out of the way;
> father and son go in to the same girl,

so that my holy name is profaned;
they lay themselves down beside every altar
    on garments taken in pledge;
and in the house of their God they drink
    wine bought with fines they imposed. (Amos 2:6–8)

Later Amos declares that while there are these social crimes taking place, where there are these injustices found in the dealings of peoples and leaders, and in particular when those who have money are not seeking to assist those who do not, then there is indeed great offence against God, as the following passage makes clear:

Hate evil and love good,
    and establish justice in the gate;
it may be that the LORD, the God of hosts,
    will be gracious to the remnant of Joseph. (Amos 5:15)

In matters like these the prophet is very much commenting upon what may indeed be regarded as a political matter. Yet for this prophet, and for others of the Hebrew prophets, clearly maintaining justice and righteousness in the society of the day is understood to be a matter of deep *religious* concern, so that there is inevitably a relationship between what we would perhaps refer to as the two realms of religion and politics. Indeed, for Amos—and for others of the Hebrew prophets—that there is justice and righteousness in the society of their day is a vital factor if the worship offered by the members of that society is to be acceptable to God. (See Amos 5:21–24). Indeed further, where there is no justice and righteousness in the communities of the people of God, then there will be the judgment of God upon them.

This theme of the care for the less-fortunate of the Israelite society is also to be observed in the graphic account of the illicit acquiring of a vineyard by King Ahab in the days of the prophet Elijah. The ownership of the vineyard, we are told, had been in the family of Naboth for generations (see 1 Kgs 21:3–4), but possession by Ahab was engineered through the evil dealings of his wife Jezebel who arranged charges of false condemnations of the Naboth family, with the result that Naboth was indeed sentenced to death, and thus the vineyard became the king's property. However, any sense and satisfaction that King Ahab might have been feeling over his new possession of the coveted vineyard was all too soon ruined by the arrival of the prophet Elijah, and the confrontation of the king by the prophet of the Lord in the vineyard. "Have you found me, O my enemy?" said Ahab to Elijah, to which the prophet responded, "I have found you. Because you have sold yourself to do what is evil in the sight of the LORD, I will bring disaster on you . . ." (1 Kgs 21:20–21).

Thus is announced the judgment of the Lord upon this sinful acquisition by the king, who had on his side wealth and authority, and was able to take advantage of the humble status of the man Naboth who had inherited his family vineyard. We note again the delineation of sinfulness here that concerns a matter of social relations, and that this is clearly understood to be an offence against the holiness and perfection of the Lord, and will bring the divine judgment upon King Ahab. Further, to be observed once again is that the failure and sinfulness of King Ahab is not to do with what he has done or not done in the sphere of the cult, in any matters concerned with prayer or sacrifice or offering, but rather with matters about the living out of that faith in the Israelite community, in the wider life of king and people in the world.

Yet this awareness of personal guilt and therefore of the associated judgment of the Lord is also spoken about in the Old Testament, perhaps above all in Ps 51 with its profound spirit of personal confession:

> Have mercy on me, O God,
>   according to your steadfast love;
> according to your abundant mercy
>   blot out my transgressions.
> Wash me thoroughly from my iniquity,
>   and cleanse me from my sin.
> For I know my transgressions,
>   and my sin is ever before me. (Ps 51:1–3)

Yet by the end of this profound and moving psalm we read of the psalmist's confidence in the Lord's forgiveness, that is the divine deliverance of this suffering person from their deep sense of sinfulness. Before the psalm is ended we read,

> The sacrifice acceptable to God is a broken spirit;
>   a broken and contrite heart, O God, you will not despise. (Ps 51:17)

We may surely say that having prominent place in the Old Testament are these twin themes of deliverance and judgment. The Old Testament scriptures speak of the Lord's deliverance of his people, not only for people who corporately have fallen on bad times, like being forced workers in Egypt or exiles in Babylonia, or those who suffer from powerful neighbors or overlords, and even kings. Those in such situations are portrayed as being seen with care, love and concern by the Lord, who acts to help them, indeed to save them. The same goes for individual suffering, and also for afflicted individual people, for whom we read of their deliverance, and whose deliverance is frequently attributed to the intervention, the action and activity of the Lord. However, it does have to be said that in not all of the examples and occurrences of suffering spoken about in the Old Testament is there also deliverance. Some people do appear in fact *not* to be delivered, and the religious problem caused by such experiences receives some consideration in ch 6 below, which seeks to deal with issues of living in the world with continuing religious questions and problems.

Yet as we have seen there is a theme also present in the Old Testament, namely that of the Lord's judgment upon the sinfulness and failures of both individuals and also whole nations. Together, these somewhat twin themes of deliverance and judgment make up a vital part of the Old Testament's overall theme of the covenant relationship that is believed to have been established between God and his people. This means that in various ways God undertakes to guide and guard his people while they for their part are called to live lives both individually and corporately in faith and trust in the Lord, and in righteousness towards all their neighbors. Both divine deliverance and holy judgment may be said to be there at the heart of the content and message of the Old Testament.

From Texts to Spirituality

It is comparatively easy in certain parts of the contemporary Christian Church to attempt dismissal of the large number of laments, both individual and corporate, we read in the Old Testament, in particular in the book of Psalms. Perhaps to some this will seem all too much like grumbling and complaining on something of a grand scale, bringing as these compositions do none other than the Lord God into the fray. For other readers of the scriptures this part of the Old Testament will seem too much like wearing one's faith all too openly, and perhaps many a sufferer in the western Church tradition these days will rather give up their believing and practicing the faith when inexplicable sufferings come their way. Certainly there is a sense at times of the unexplainable in the face of human sufferings and setbacks in the Christian life, in no small way when it is affirmed that central to the biblical faith is that the Lord is indeed a delivering Lord. Yet, as we have seen, he is also the Lord who cannot but set his judgment upon his peoples' sins and sinfulness.

There is also, as we have seen, that prominent tradition in the Old Testament book of Psalms of crying out to God in the face and experience of some of life's inexplicable sufferings—this being both on the parts of individuals and also of whole communities, even nations. For those of us in the western traditions of the Christian Church there is a significant witness to take notice of here, that when sufferings come the way of Christians, either singly or corporately the response of ceasing to join in worship, and even in effect of renouncing faith and belief in God, does not have to be the only way for the present and the future. Rather, as we observed, the Hebrew scriptures witness to a tradition of crying out to God, at times in a mood and intensity of urgent need of help. This may even be with a clear element of anger, that this must be happening to one—or even to a community— that is seeking faithfully to follow the revealed way of the Lord. Yet, as again we have seen, so often by the end of such psalms the psalmist has come to a sense of peace and quietness—how and in what ways we are not told, and nor do we know. But we do find a profound sense of holy peace, and the apparent strength to go on with life. Does not the Old Testament have something to say to us here about the fact that it proclaims the Lord who is to be found and experienced as a delivering Lord?

The Old Testament surely also speaks to us about the judgment of the Lord upon our sinfulness, and also upon those sins that daily and weekly we commit. It is surely appropriate that in our public liturgies and private devotions we should give space and time to making our confessions, humbly asking for the divine forgiveness, and seeking for a renewal of our spiritual lives. Further, we should not forget that emphasis in the Old Testament that not all our sins are to do with our liturgies and devotions, either their quantities or their contents, but that perhaps to be taken the more seriously—or at least equally seriously—are those sins committed in our daily lives in our secular communities and in the whole life of the world, that there in particular we should be doing justice and loving mercy as well as seeking to walk humbly with our Lord (see Mic 6:8).

There is surely a place in the corporate Christian life for the voice of the Lord to be heard about our sinfulness, both individual and corporate, the latter of which may perforce lead us into the political arena, and to the making of judgments upon some of the decisions of the politicians. The prophet Elijah certainly demonstrates to us how the unjust use of power by national authority needs to be challenged by religious leaders! We also hear this in the proclamations of others of the Old Testament prophets, and we may well wonder if we do hear it sufficiently in the Church in our contemporary world. Surely those twin Old Testament themes of the ongoing divine deliverance of those who are suffering, and also judgment upon those who in sinful ways act in the world, need still to be heard in our world today, and call to have a place in the Christian spiritualities of individual

Christians and also of their Churches—local, national and international. With a deep sense of real spiritual longing do we pray for a day when for all the peoples there will be justice and peace, life and caring consideration, righteousness and wholeness.

Meanwhile, as far as individuals are concerned, in this matter of the living out of their Christian spirituality, and seeking to the best of their prayers and abilities to live out the life of faith in, and faithfulness to, the Lord, might usefully heed the words of that spiritual guide, Thomas à Kempis, who sought to offer comfort and counsel in the following words:

> I have never found anyone so religious and devout who did not on occasion experience withdrawal of grace, or sense a cooling of ardour. No saint was so enraptured or enlightened, who was not sooner or later tempted. For he is not worthy of lofty contemplation of God, who for God's sake is not exercised by some tribulation. For temptation commonly goes before as a sign of consolation which shall follow. For heaven's consolation is promised to those proved by temptations. "To him that overcomes," he says, "I will give to eat of the tree of life."

Yet indeed, there is much that the Old Testament can contribute to our Christian spirituality, both for individuals and also for communities in these matters of divine deliverance and human sinfulness, of divine judgment and the Lord's deliverance.

3

Life of Worship

> For his sovereignty is an everlasting sovereignty,
>   and his kingdom endures from generation to generation.
> All the inhabitants of the earth are accounted as nothing,
>   and he does what he wills with the host of heaven
>   and the inhabitants of the earth. (Dan 4:34b–35a)

THUS WE ARE TOLD Nebuchadnezzar, king of Babylon, came to express his praise of the Most High God—and Daniel's God. Indeed, in the book of Daniel there are various other expressions of the praise of the Lord God, for example in Dan 4:3, 37; 6:26–27; 7:14. More, throughout the whole of the Old Testament a good deal is spoken about worship, there being in fact few books of the whole having no mention of the subject. By the end of the historical Old Testament period there will have been much written about shrines and temples, and about those who were responsible for the maintenance of the worship within them, in particular the priests and the Levites. Moreover, it is here that we find the Bible's large collection of psalms, which generation upon generation of Christians have found helpful, and that could readily to be taken into and used in their own worship, study and thinking.

The mention of priests and Levites may give rise to a certain impatience on the part of Christian readers, for particularly in such books as Leviticus—the mass of what is believed to be "priestly" material, that is, written matter which seems to reflect the concerns of priests—these may seem to be about issues that Christians could easily leave behind, or at least regard as being of secondary importance, concerns that might without great loss be left on one side. Still, there was a vital ministry in ancient Israel conducted by the priests, along with what appears to have been the assistance of the Levites, in a particular way in connection with the operation of the sacrificial system. For the sacrifices in all their variety, were believed to have been a divine gift of the means whereby a people who had accidentally sinned might have their sins forgiven. Thus there was a range of sacrifices for a gamut of sins and settings, for this was believed to be the means whereby certain of the sinful people might be restored to fellowship with their holy God.

Yet the Old Testament knows of other means whereby sins may be forgiven, such as prayers of confession, an example of which is the extended prayer of dedication of the Jerusalem Temple by King Solomon (see 1 Kgs 8:22–61). Or a Moses might make a prayer requesting the Lord to forgive his people a grave sin (Exod 32:11–14, 30–32), or a prophet, or the prophet's editor, might make a bold statement about their belief in the Lord God of Israel, that he is the God who forgives his people their sins (Mic 7:18–20). So also in a psalm could a prayer be suggested whereby a sinner might in penitence come to the Lord and pray him to forgive their sins, as for example with Ps 51.

The mention of a psalm reminds us that in the Old Testament's book of psalms we do have a large collection of material that is surely *worship material*. The psalms in all their varieties of feelings and portrayed situations give to us a whole range of hymns and prayers, expressions of wonder, praise and celebration; they give us intercessions, petitions, even serious complaints with outspokenness to God concerning all that a person or a group (or the psalmist?) is passing through and thus involving them in inexplicably difficult and testing times. Such psalms may sometimes include the element of protest about these strange and unexpected happenings. Further, while such expressions of anguish do not come through to any theological "solution" to the problem, yet so often they come to a spirit of contentment, satisfaction, above all to new expressions of confidence in the Lord, as for example in the closing words of Psalm 73 (see especially vv. 23–26). Yet these various aspects of, and concerns about, worship are to be found not only in the large book of Psalms, but also in many other parts of the Old Testament, in the notes of praise and thanksgiving, confession, prayers in a whole variety of situations and concerns, expressions of dedication and renewal.

Moreover, the Old Testament has a good deal to say about the place and places of worship, that is the setting where it is intended worship should take place. So it speaks of tents, tabernacles, shrines, and temples—not forgetting either individual homes as places of worship, or those forbidden places where the Israelites are commanded *not* to worship, such as on (the Canaanite) high places and under green trees (see for example 1 Kgs 3:3,

4; 2 Kgs 17:9–11; 18:4), for fear of the worshippers being contaminated by the non-Yahwistic worship as practiced by the Canaanites. For in the Old Testament there are perceived to be adequate and appropriate places of worship, holy places where there might be a meeting of God and his people, and places too that with their various furnishings, appurtenances and contents speak eloquently of the things of God, those holy things that were inevitably in fact matters invisible. Thus do humans need their temples and shrines to be in the nature of "non-verbal signs" of their Lord and of the things of their faith.

Still there is more in the Old Testament about worship, such as that emphasis in Deuteronomy about keeping worship pure, true and uncorrupted by what may be contrary forces, influences, suggestions in the world around. Then in the books of Chronicles, particularly in the second of these, there are examples of joyful worship, the singing of psalms, and the use of musical instruments in worship. Above all, this worship about which the Old Testament speaks is a reaching out of creatures of earth to their Lord who is believed to be their Creator, their Sustainer, their Lord and their Guide.

Further, in various places there are set out in the Old Testament books a series of feasts, festivals, and calendars, which perhaps usefully serve to remind us that the worship "year" is intended to have some shape, logic, and progression. In this regard see especially Exod 12:1–13; 23:14–17; 34:18–26; Lev 23:1–44; Num 28:1–29:40; Deut 16:1–17. Yet whatever is done by way of worship in this season or in that, there is surely in these Old Testament scriptures the praise of a grateful people for their Lord's guidance and deliverance in the past days and months, and at the same time in their divinely-given covenant relationship the humble and prayerful seeking of the continuation of that same guidance and divine blessing for the coming days.

In the Old Testament there are various styles, or what we might call "types," of worship, which I shall examine below, namely what I would call Priestly, Deuteronomic, Psalmic, Expressions of awe, and Worship centered on sacred documents. First, then, we turn to the style of worship in the Old Testament that has been labelled "Priestly."

What we mean by the "Priestly" style of worship, is that worship which in the main is spoken about in parts of the book of Exodus, in the book of Leviticus, and in parts of the book of Numbers. This is all material that in a general sense gives the impression that it has been compiled and written by priests, for the purpose of conveying to priests how they should go about their priestly work and duties. This style of worship was centered to a large degree upon sacrifices, especially in the matter of offering the correct sacrifice for the particular occasion, and how that sacrifice was to be offered.

What these documents make clear is that the religious purpose of the offerings of sacrifices was to secure the forgiveness of sins, though just how this was actually effected we are not told. What is clearer is that the blood of the main sacrifices was significant, though once again why it was, is never explained. Perhaps the priestly writers assumed that their readers knew, or at least had some sort of intuition about, the answers to these things. What, however, comes through with some clarity is that the blood had a crucial role in the sacrificing of an offering, we being told in Lev 17:11, though once again any questions we may have about "how" and "why" are not answered,

> For the life of the flesh is in the blood; and I have given it to you for making atonement for your lives on the altar; for, as life, it is the blood that makes atonement.

We should take note of the fact that in our Old Testament studies we have in recent decades been helped by various anthropological investigations into the religious rites of some ancient societies in various parts of the world. For it is clear that many ancient societies offered sacrifices, these being offered so as, among other things, to secure the avoidance of punishment, and the forgiveness of sins. The Old Testament shares something of this belief, acknowledging that here was a great and divine gift that the Lord's people on earth had been given whereby in an ever-mysterious way they could secure, and be assured of, the forgiveness of their sins. What however we cannot know is *how* it could be believed that thereby sins would be forgiven. Nevertheless, there was not forgiveness here for *all* sins, but rather of accidental sins, sins not intended by a person, or group, or tribe, or nation. Even so there were other ways—as for example through prayers of contrition and confession—that deliberate sins ("sins committed with a high hand") could be forgiven. See for example the moving confession of a psalmist in Psalm 51, and once again the long prayer prayed by King Solomon on what we are told was the occasion of the dedication of the Jerusalem temple, which was a humble plea for forgiveness of a whole wide range of sins (1 Kgs 8:22–53).

The book of Leviticus speaks about burnt offerings, in which almost the whole of the animal was burnt on the altar (Lev 1:1–7), of grain offerings (2:1–16), of sin offerings (4:1—5:13), of guilt offerings (5:14–16 and 7:1–6), and the particular reasons for each of these is more clearly seen in some cases than in others. Things are, however, clearer when we come to Lev 16 and the detailed instructions therein concerning the Day of Atonement. This is clearly portrayed as a most solemn day in the liturgical calendar for the people of Israel, in which both burnt and sin offerings were made, and in which also one of two goats was sent away into the wilderness symbolically bearing the sins of the people. This latter also is a rite that is known to have taken place in many ancient religious cultures. Further, we today can speak of a "scapegoat," namely, one person who bears the blame due to others.

It is perhaps tempting for Christians to regard these sacrificial rites as those of a religion of long ago, and now that Christ has come have been rendered outmoded and no longer appropriate. Yet we may keep in mind two considerations. In the first place it is certainly so that the New Testament understands that in Christ something has taken place of a most decisive nature about human sinfulness and divine forgiveness of sins. Yet some of the New Testament writers use the Old Testament language of sin and forgiveness to express the new thing that has taken place, as for example, in the First Letter of Peter, the Letter to the Hebrews, and in what looks like the understanding of the author of the fourth Gospel expressed in the announcement of John the Baptist, "Look, here is the Lamb of God!" (John 1:36). In the second place we may wish to consider how the sacrificial system in ancient Israel might have given a real sense of assurance to the worshippers and offerers of those days, by the very fact that they could see something happening about the wretched matter of their sins and their sheer proneness to sinfulness, that they could themselves touch and handle their offerings, be given something visible and tangible to "speak" of sins being *taken away,* forgiven; that there was indeed something here being enacted that might give to them the assurance of sins forgiven.

We may proceed to consider another type, or style, of worship that is found in the Old Testament, namely what we may call Deuteronomic (that is in the style, the language, and the religious approach of the book of Deuteronomy), and that is to be found in the so-called Deuteronomic literature of the Hebrew Bible, that is the book of Deuteronomy along with those books that evidence the deuteronomistic influence upon them, in particular in the books of Samuel and the books of Kings. A distinctive feature of these writings is their portrayal of a holy nation which had failed to offer pure worship to the Lord. In particular, their priests, prophets, kings and people had allowed themselves and their worship of the Lord God to become corrupted by their neighbors' words and rituals. Thus, for example, the writers of these documents stress the horrors of offering human sacrifices as possibly some of the people of Israel's neighbors did. There was also Canaanite worship that took place on what are called "high places," and other such worship "under green trees." These were ways and practices that the people of Israel and their leaders were to shun completely.

The so-called Deuteronomic writers in fact had a very radical solution to this particular problem, namely that of laying down that worship was to be offered only at the one central place appointed by the Lord. This seems to have been the temple in Jerusalem, but no doubt this "solution" was both too radical and also largely impracticable. There must have been many an Israelite who quite simply could not physically make the journey to Jerusalem! Thus perhaps Deuteronomy laid down that all Israelite people should *once a year* worship in the central shrine in Jerusalem, that is at the Temple on Mount Zion, and those psalms with the titles "Song of Ascents" (Pss 120–34) were perhaps for the use of, encouragement of, indeed the worship such pilgrims might offer on their journeys to and from, as well as at the temple. Undoubtedly this deuteronomistic regulation about the sole and central sanctuary as a place for worship will seem to present day Christian readers of the Old Testament to be harsh and impracticable, but the principle it enshrined, and its apparent original purpose, may present us with some appropriate challenges about our worship of God in our contemporary settings and about the contents and emphases of that worship.

The book of Deuteronomy, and also the so-called deuteronomistic literature, has a quite distinctive way of speaking about the presence of God in the earthly place of worship. The writers of these works would appear to insist that the Lord does not live, actually dwell in such places—presumably for the reason that they believed that he was just too great and "other" than human beings to do so, and thus they spoke of the place where the Lord had chosen to "put his name" (see Deut 12:11, 21; 14:23, 24; 16:2, 6, 11; 26:2). That is to say, presumably these writers wished to speak about a spiritual, rather than about any rather crudely physical, presence of the Lord in the earthly sanctuary and with his people. The Lord was possessed of an especial *otherness* from the humans; in his greatness he was truly a *spiritual* being. Further, his people on earth in age after age were therefore called to have what we today might call a *spiritual aspect* to their lives

This deuteronomic emphasis upon the spiritual presence of the Lord in these earthly sanctuaries is also to be seen in the deuteronomistic literature, as that embraces the theological emphases of the book of Deuteronomy. The clearest case of this is in the books of Kings, and here there is indeed emphasis on the fact that the temple is the "dwelling place for the LORD's name" (as in 1 Kgs 8:16; 11:36; 14:21; 2 Kgs 21:7; 23:27), but certainly not the (physical) dwelling place of God. There is also in these deuteronomistic books an emphasis upon a sole, single place of worship, and thus for these theologians the very model of good kingship was to be seen and demonstrated in the reign of good King Josiah, who sought to give effect to this demand that there be a sole place of worship, namely the temple in Jerusalem (2 Kgs 23:8–9).

For the book of Deuteronomy and those books that espouse the deuteronomic theological emphases worship is the glad celebration of all that the Lord has done for his people, and still does do for them and in their midst (see Deut 12:7; 14:22–27; 26:11). There is no very great emphasis here upon the institution of sacrifice, but there is, for example in the long prayer of King Solomon at the dedication of the temple in Jerusalem, a real emphasis on prayer (see 1 Kgs 8:1–53)—here the temple is portrayed as the people's place of prayer.

Another of the Old Testament's style, or types, of worship is what we might call the Psalmic, and of course its great witness to us is in the Old Testament's large book of psalms, and also among those various psalm-like compositions we encounter in other parts of these scriptures, such as Jonah 2:1–10; Nah 1:2–11 and Hab 3:1–19. This is written matter that does have the appearance of being intended for the world of worship. It is not writings about *how* a people found themselves in this situation and *how* they later came to be in that situation. Nor is it material that sets forth the Lord's words, either of judgment or of comfort, to his people. Rather, here are clearly *words for worship*, and they are words that come in a series of compositions giving the clear impression of being intended for the various stages of worship, and that will also take into account the differing moods, situations, blessings, misfortunes, pains and sins of the worshippers. If we consider the various movements, parts of an act of worship, thinking of this as either corporate or as individual, we may at the same time consider a number of "types" of psalms that match these movements.

In the first place we may first think of two types of the biblical psalms that are about the *preparatory stages* on the way to worship. The first of these is a small group of just two psalms, 15 and 24, but along with these we may note the similar wording in Isa 33:14–16. These texts are concerned with the sense of unworthiness, of sinfulness on the part of the worshippers, but the unworthiness is not in any way about correctness in religious devotions, but rather is about how the worshipper has lived in the world, how the worshipper has treated neighbors and friends. Here is something by way of a personal and individual spiritual examination before we seek to worship the Lord, something we might think of as an Entrance Liturgy.

Then there is a group of psalms that are *hymns of praise*, the first of these being Ps 8 but in all they total nearly forty, some of them being in a series of small blocks (Pss 95–100, 134–136, 145–150). These psalms set forth the praise of God in unbounded terms, as we observe in Ps 8 with its words "O Lord, our Sovereign, how majestic is your name in all the earth" framing the whole composition in its appearance both at the beginning and at the end (vv. 1a and 9). Between these poles, this psalm sets forth the wonder of the Lord, in particular of his work of creating on the one hand the heavens and the earth (vv. 1b–2), and on the other the remarkable, responsible and privileged place given to the human beings in this creation (vv. 3–8). Yet this is only the first of the psalter's expressions of the praise and adoration of the great Lord of all.

Further, we should consider the aspect of *confession of sins*, a movement in worship which naturally follows on from the Entrance Liturgy and the Psalm of Praise. This theme of confession we find above all in such psalms as Pss 6, 32, 38, 51, 102 and 143, and these have been called Penitential Psalms by some parts of the Christian Church. We may consider Ps 51 as an example of this group, for here the psalmist's sense of unworthiness and his obviously heartfelt confession of sin are profound and moving, the psalmist pleading with God to have mercy upon him. All that the psalmist can ask is that God will treat him with "steadfast love," and in accordance with his abundant mercy blot out the psalmist's transgressions (Ps 51:1).

However, there are other psalms—in fact many psalms—in which a psalmist makes a moving appeal to God about the difficulties he is experiencing in his life. These psalms have been called *lament psalms*, and they come in two main groups, what have been called the Individual Laments, and the Communal Laments. The Individual Laments are the most numerous, that frequency being at its greatest in the earlier parts of the Psalter. Further, these lament psalms occur much less frequently as we go on through the whole book—so that, as we have seen, the whole work ends on the note of praise in the block of psalmic hymns (Pss 145–150). We find these Individual Laments in the First Book of the Psalter (Pss 1–72) at Pss 3–7; 9/10; 13; 17; 22; 25–28; 31; 35; 38–39; 40:13–17=70; 42/43; 51–52; 54–57; 59; 61; 64; 69–71, and they continue on, though with decreasing frequency, in the Second to Fifth Books of the Psalter.

In these Individual Lament psalms the psalmist cries out to God, sometimes as if in agony, oftentimes with a real note of anger that God is letting the psalmist suffer so much. Yet the crucial fact is that although things are going so badly for this individual, yet that individual clings onto God, at times calling upon God in very strong language to bring about a change in this suffering person's life. What is surely crucial to note about this is the fact that the suffering psalmist does not "give up" on God; rather the psalmist demands an answer, and above all a change in the experience of living earthly life. Further, frequently there is a change by the end of these psalms, strongly suggesting that the psalmist has come to a state of calm and sense of peace; and then there is the note of the praise of the Lord.

There is also in the book of psalms a much less numerous group of what have been called Communal Laments in which a group, or indeed the whole nation, is portrayed as crying out to God in their suffering and agonies. Communal Laments are found at Pss 12; 44; 60; 74; 79; 80; 83; 85;

94:1–11; 126, while Isa 63:7–64:11; Jer 14:2–9, 19–22 and Lam 5 do appear to be similar reflections upon like situations. We read in the Old Testament of days of national mourning (see, for example, 1 Sam 7:6; Jer 14), and perhaps these psalms were used on such, and no doubt other, occasions when people were facing up to setbacks, military defeats, or other national, or at least corporate, calamities.

Now for something different. In the book of psalms there is a group of psalms that Old Testament scholars are reasonably united in calling "Royal Psalms," but at the same time are divided about just which, and how many of the individual psalms belong to this category. These psalms concern the Israelite king, and it may be that some of them were in the nature of being "Coronation Psalms," Ps 2 possibly being one of these. Others were concerned with the high and important office the king had, in particular that under God he was called not only to protect his people from their enemies, but also that he would ensure justice and righteousness among them, and in particular that suitable provision was made so that there was justice for those who did not have power and influence. Thus in Ps 72 there is the prayer that the king may have serious regard for those who are poor and needy: "May he defend the cause of the poor of the people, give deliverance to the needy, and crush the oppressor." (v. 4) Psalm 45 looks as if it was in the nature of a song—or perhaps we might describe it as an "anthem"?—for the occasion of the marriage of a king, in which the praise of God is set forth, and at the same time prayer is made for the reigning earthly king and for his queen. May this king "ride on victoriously for the cause of truth and to defend the right." (Ps 45:4) In Ps 89 we have a hymn of praise to God, including the words, "I will establish your descendants forever, and build your throne for all generations" (v. 4), and which at the same time prays for a king who is experiencing difficulties in the exercise of his high calling, "Lord, where is your steadfast love of old, which by your faithfulness you swore to David?" (v. 49).

Then another group of psalms has been called "Wisdom Psalms" for the reason that they are asking questions about the meaning of life, in particular what can be said from the religious point of view about the sufferings that some believing people experience at certain times. Such psalms are 37, 49, and 73, and it has to be said that none of these psalms expresses anything by way of an adequate answer to this deep and perplexing problem, but at least the issue has been raised and the problem has been aired, as also it is in other parts of the Old Testament. We shall return to this subject in ch 6, but for the meantime we may take note of the fact that while the main part of Ps 73 deals with the inexplicable facts of suffering, yet the psalmist is able to end his composition with a moving expression of confidence in the Lord's ever-constant presence with him:

> Nevertheless I am continually with you;
>   you hold my right hand.
> You guide me with your counsel,
>   and afterwards you will receive me with honor.
> Whom have I in heaven but you?
>   And there is nothing on earth that I desire other than you.
> My flesh and my heart may fail,
>   but God is the strength of my heart and my portion forever.
> (Ps 73:23–26)

Another group of psalms is those that have been labelled Confidence Psalms, such as Ps 11, and perhaps supremely Ps 23, "The LORD is my shepherd, I shall not want," with its most confident statement about a worst-case scenario, which is perhaps to say either a hardly-believable calamity or even death itself,

> Even though I walk through the darkest valley,
>   I fear no evil;
> for you are with me;
>   your rod and your staff—
>   they comfort me. (Ps 23:4)

This is a remarkable and moving statement of confident faith that surely was used by the peoples of Old Testament times, by members of the Jewish faith and also by Christian congregations and individuals. We shall consider this psalm further in ch 8 below.

There are other types of the biblical psalms that should be mentioned, albeit briefly, such as a series of thanksgivings, examples being Pss 32 and 34, psalms that express a developed degree of thanksgiving for the Lord's deliverances from this trouble and that, as we find for example in Ps 34:6 "This poor soul cried, and was heard by the LORD, and was saved from every trouble." Other psalms have words reminding us of the proclamations of the prophets, and which thus have been called "Prophetic," such as Pss 52, 58, 81. Some psalms are of mixed type, such as Ps 27, while the long Ps 119 very much gives the impression of being something in the nature of a literary *tour de force* on an acrostic literary arrangement, each group of verses beginning on the succeeding letter of the (Hebrew) alphabet.

Here then, in the biblical Psalter is a remarkable and varied resource of material that was manifestly intended to be for use in worship. At the same time a good number of the questions we have about this worship material remain unanswered. We note that the book of Psalms is divided into Five Books, but in spite of theories that have been propounded about these "books" not all of us are convinced about suggested solutions as to the significance of this division of the psalter. Nor do we have the necessary information to interpret and understand the significance of the various headings to the psalms, these having been attached to already existing psalms, such as, for example, the "To the leader: according to The Gittith" of Pss 8, 81 and 84. And still the word "Selah" occurring as it does with frequency in the Psalter eludes us as to its meaning and significance. It gives us the impression that it is a liturgical instruction of some sort. Further, we know remarkably little about the various musical instruments spoken about, apart from hazarding guesses that they are instruments either of percussion, or string, or wind varieties.

There is, however, one aspect of worship that we find, maybe surprisingly, largely absent in the Psalter is that involving sacrifice. The fact is that sacrifice is remarkably infrequently spoken of in the Psalter, and perhaps we have simply to say that here in the psalms is material for non-sacrificial worship. Yet it should be further observed that this psalmic material has been found by individuals and groups, large and small, of Old Testament, Jewish and Christian worshippers, to be a great treasure and resource for their own worship, and moreover to be for their generations of worshippers a great source and resource for their spirituality and spiritual growth.

So to another of the aspects of the worship we read about in the pages of the Old Testament, and this I refer to as an *aspect* rather than a style or a type for the reason that it is a characteristic feature of a number of the narrated encounters of people with the Lord in which there is a real sense of the *awesomeness* of the moment of this meeting of the indescribably great and holy Lord on the one side, while on the part of a sinful person of earth, a grave feeling of unworthiness, inadequacy, sinfulness. Thus, for example, in the encounter of the young Moses and the Lord at the site of the burning bush on Mount Horeb we read of the Lord calling to Moses out of the burning bush, "Moses, Moses! . . . Come no closer! Remove the sandals from your feet, for the place on which you are standing is holy ground." We then read "And Moses hid his face, for he was afraid to look at God." (Exod 3:4–6)

And that word translated "afraid" should surely be understood in the sense that Moses was filled with a sense of *holy awe* as he found himself in the very near presence of the Lord God. As we have seen the same Hebrew word has both of these meanings, namely feeling *afraid* and feeling a *sense of awe*. In parts of the Old Testament we read of certain individuals having a mighty experience of the Lord, what has been called a "theophany," an appearance, that is of God, of a deity, and we can well believe that some such places became places of pilgrimage and worship for later generations. See, for example, Gen 28:10–22.

Such an experience of the meeting of the holy and the sinful is also sensed in the account of the encounter on the same mountain of Moses and Aaron, Nadab, and Abihu, and seventy of the elders of Israel with the Lord, when we read concerning the holy Lord, "Under his feet there was something like a pavement of sapphire stone, like the very heaven for clearness" (Exod 24:10). A few verses later we further read, "Now the appearance of the glory of the Lord was like a devouring fire on the top of the mountain in the sight of the people of Israel." (v. 17)

Surely we have here a writer who is struggling to find adequate, suitable, appropriate earthly words to express the otherness, glory, awesomeness of the divine presence, the sheer experience of what has been called the *numinous*, what invokes within us a sense of awe. We sense the same sort of struggle with language in the account of the experience of the priest Ezekiel, the son of Buzi, in a somewhat extended narrative of the Lord's appearance to him that will lead into the call to be his prophet. One cannot help feeling that the writer here was seeking to express his deep sense of awe about this encounter with the divine:

> . . . there was something like a throne, in appearance like sapphire; and seated above the likeness of a throne was something like a human form. Upward from what appeared like the loins I saw something like gleaming amber, something that looked like fire enclosed all around; and downward from what looked like the loins I saw something that looked like fire, and there was a splendor all around. Like the bow in a cloud on a rainy day, such was appearance of the splendor all around. This was the appearance of the likeness of the glory of the Lord. When I saw it, I fell on my face, and I heard the voice of someone speaking. (Ezek 1:26–28)

Again it is there in the quiet and devout responses of the man Job who in his earlier speeches is portrayed as being at times remarkably outspoken to the Lord, and also about the Lord, yet when that Lord appears to Job and speaks to him, how humble—and humbled—he is:

> See, I am of small account; what shall I answer you?
>   I lay my hand on my mouth.
> I have spoken once, and I will not answer;
>   twice, but will proceed no further. (Job 40:4–5)

Or consider those so-called Doxologies of Amos, expressions of awesome praise of the Lord into which the prophet in his book from time to time breaks,

> For lo, the one who forms the mountains, creates the wind,
> reveals his thoughts to mortals,
> makes the morning darkness,
> and treads on the heights of the earth—
> the Lord, the God of hosts, is his name! (Amos 4:13. See also
> 5:8–9; 9:5–6.)

This is surely an aspect of the worship of God that calls for emulation by the Christians in their worship, this worshipful acknowledgement of the awesomeness of God, perhaps, for example, as they recall something of that sense of amazement and wonder expressed by the author of the Gospel of St John, "And the Word became flesh and lived among us, and we have seen his glory, the glory as of a father's only son, full of grace and truth." (John 1:14)

There is just one more approach to worship, style of worship, occurring but briefly in the Old Testament of which we should take note. However, history makes it clear that much was to come out of this but once-recorded incident, an incident we are told taking place in the time when in the post-exilic period Jewish life was being restored in Jerusalem and the surrounding countryside. According to Neh 8:1–18, the people of Jerusalem were gathered together into the square before the Water Gate, and the scribe Ezra brought to them what is described as "the book of the law of Moses, which the Lord had given to Israel." (Neh 8:1) This we assume was material that had been compiled during the days of exile, and that became the beginnings of, part of, what would eventuate as the Torah, the Pentateuch, the first five books of the Hebrew Bible and the Christians' Bible. At any rate, we are told that Ezra stood on a wooden platform, with some ceremony opening the book, whereupon the people stood up, and Ezra having blessed the Lord, and the people lifting up their hands and worshipping the Lord with their faces to the ground, Ezra read from the document. The Levites appear to have had a significant role, for we are told that they helped the people to *understand* the law, while the people remained in their places (Neh 8:4–7). That is, so we read, "So they read from the book, from the law of God, with interpretation. They gave the sense, so that the people understood the reading." (Neh 8:8)

In later times this style of worship, in which scriptures are read with some real sense of solemnity before a congregation, and then expounded, interpreted, so that many may understand the reading, or readings, would become widespread and common. Indeed, what evolved as the sermon based upon a biblical passage or verse would occupy different lengths of time depending upon the particular church tradition of worship. Yet one cannot help but feel that what we read about in the book of Neh 8 is portrayed as the small beginnings of something that would blossom and burgeon into a very large and significant part both of Jewish and also Christian worship.

What, then, can we say can we say about the *place* of worship, the holy place, about the chosen settings for the practicing of these various styles, types, of worship about which the Old Testament documents speak? It is clear that although a person or a group can worship and pray in any setting, yet there is a real sense of importance attached to the dedicated holy place as a chosen setting for worship. In the patriarchal narratives in the book of Genesis we have what is portrayed as the beginnings of this, for we read of ancestors setting up stones of remembrance for mercies and revelations received, such as Jacob on the morning after his dream at Bethel (Gen 28:18–19), or an altar may have been built (Gen 8:20–21). Later we read of shrines being built in the land (for example Gen 12:6–7; 26:23–25), and there was even what is called a temple in Shiloh in the days of Eli and the young Samuel (1 Sam 3).

Further, in the book of Exodus, as we have already seen, there are accounts not only of a simple tent for the meeting of individuals with the Lord in prayer (Exod 33:7–11; Num 11:16–30; 12:1–16), but there are also copious details both in the specification of, and also the building of, a much larger sanctuary, called the tabernacle (Exod 35:1—40:38), which as we have observed are remarkably similar to what we are told was later built in Jerusalem, so that many of us understand that these are indeed details of what was eventually built as the temple in Jerusalem, but that here have been retrojected, cast back, set back, into the desert setting. Thus was emphasized that the later Jerusalem temple was built in accordance with the details and instructions given to the earthly leader Moses by none other than God "on the mountain" that is Horeb/Sinai (Exod 25:40; 26:30; 27:8).

The Jerusalem temple was built in the days of the kingship of Solomon, and clearly became something of a wonder of its age, a place of religious pilgrimage, a holy place where it was believed the presence of the Lord was to be sought, and where he was to be worshipped. Certainly there was much of value, not only in monetary terms but also as regards what the whole edifice stood for in matters of religious belief, in that building with all its various religious artefacts. Understandably, there was a profound religious crisis when that temple was destroyed in 587 BCE by the Babylonian army, and it is more than understandable that in later times, in the days after Israelites were allowed to return to Jerusalem and Judah, there should have been urgent calls from prophets such as Haggai that a new Jerusalem temple should be built as a matter of urgency (Hag 1:7–14).

Yet, we may ask, why was there such an elaborate temple in Jerusalem, and why were there those other shrines and temples we have considered? Surely they were intended to be dedicated buildings which by their sheer and imposing presence spoke of the reality of the Lord's constant presence in delivering power, to present *visually* something of his divine purposes for his people and his world. Further, these vital matters would be set forth in the rites and ceremonies enacted in this holy place, both in words and in actions. How else could these people of old, and also we ourselves today, be assured and reassured of God's presence without the help of visible buildings with their various artefacts and furnishings that went at least some way to set forth various aspects of the invisible relationship of the human peoples with the divine and holy one? Many no doubt will have believed that God had made his dwelling there, and thus was indeed *with* his people. Those responsible for the book of Deuteronomy made it clear that for them it was inadmissible to speak of the great, eternal, and spiritual being of God being actually *physically* present there. Rather, they wished to say that the Lord had "caused his name" to dwell there in the temple (Deut 12:11, 21; 14:23, 24; 16:2, 6, 11), which is perhaps to say in the language of today that the Lord was *spiritually* present there in the holy place.

There were, however, in the Old Testament era a number of places of worship other than these official shrines and the temple. It would certainly seem that worship took place in homes, though we have sparse details of this. There were other places of worship clearly frequented by Israelite peoples which were condemned by their leaders, in particular the Canaanite "high places," and shrines "under green trees." A succession of Judean kings sought to bring Israelite involvement in such centres of worship to an end, but the continued references to them indicates that that involvement did still take place. Further, at some time late in the Old Testament era, some time before the days of the Christians, there arose the institution of the Synagogue where worship was focussed very considerably upon written documents, a style of worship that we have earlier observed is portrayed as taking its rise in the proclamation of the book of the law of Moses spoken about in ch 8 of the book of Nehemiah, and mentioned above. And, of course, one could worship the Lord anywhere, perhaps either where a person had received a mercy or a deliverance, or else when on a journey—and such a traveller could, if they wished, and thinking it would be helpful, in the moment of prayer turn and face towards Jerusalem and all that great building there that represented, even perhaps "spoke" of all that divine sacredness and holiness (see 1 Kgs 8:30, 42, 44).

From Texts to Spirituality

Worship constitutes one of the major themes in the Old Testament and there is material on this subject that is reasonably straightforward for Christians to take and read, and also to use in their worship. The obvious part of the Old Testament in this regard is the large and varied book of psalms, Christians having found here material that has served them through many centuries of the worship life of the Church. Here Christians have materials that provide a large source, with reasonably straightforward access, that are appropriate for a wide variety of seasons and days in the liturgical calendar, and also for both corporate and individual needs in a variety of situations from the most joyous to the sad and even tragic.

The Psalter's contents, for example, have been used by Christians in a whole variety of ways through the centuries of the Church, as the recent work of Susan Gillingham helpfully sets forth. For psalms have been set in various ages and their differing styles of worship, in anthems and oratorios; in other cases providing hymns for Christians to sing, such as Martin Luther's (1483–1546) "Out of the depths I cry to thee" (Ps 130); John Milton's (1608–74) "The LORD will come, and not be slow" (Pss 82, 85, 86); Nahum Tate (1652–1715) and Nicholas Brady's (1659–1726) "Through all the changing scenes of life"; more recently in the worship compositions from the community at Taizé; and in so many other examples of Christian worship.

There are also surely a goodly number of further resources for Christian worship within the pages of the Old Testament, for example in those parts that are grappling with issues of unexplained and seemingly unexplainable suffering, or as a reminder that here are so many recorded prayers to God from a whole wide range of situations. Here in the Old Testament is set forth something of the great mystery of the awesome God who can be prayed to by any person about any issue, even on any occasion.

Also among the helpful Old Testament worship materials is the considerable emphasis on the holy place, whether that be with no more than a standing stone, a stone of remembrance, or else a building dedicated to praise and prayer, worship, and contemplation. There is surely much here to assist Christians as they seek to pinpoint, understand, and give expression to their own reasons why holy places are needed, how they can speak to us about the mysterious and unexplainable aspects of faith, and provide conducive and dedicated places for worship, fellowship, and new experiences and understandings of Christian spirituality.

Here further is material about worship centered upon sacred documents, about seeking the divine in worship, finding help in matters to do with the numinous, the holy, the other. Here are places that may help to lead people either to the straightforward aspects of Christian faith, while at the same time being there to help and guide them to artefacts, experiences, texts and stories that will perhaps be of assistance in those times of difficulty through which all people pass at various stages in their lives.

At the same time it does have to be said that there are parts of the Old Testament dealing with worship that do present certain difficulties for Christians. There are, in the first place, those imprecatory parts of certain of the psalms, where prayers are made that various people may be recipients of the judgment of God; when a grim and grisly fate is prayerfully wished upon certain individuals or groups. Christians have been told to love their enemies and pray for those who persecute them (Matt 5:44). There is here a seriously acknowledged problem with certain parts of the Old Testament, and perhaps all that we can do is simply not turn to such parts of the Old Testament in our liturgical practices. Already, this is the practice in certain of the Christian Churches' current lectionaries.

Perhaps another area of problems in the Old Testament materials for some Christians is a certain prevalence of, and emphasis upon, sacrifices with the associated talk of blood. Here we should perhaps be using such materials to quicken our awareness of the depth of feeling and concern there is in the Old Testament about the whole matter of the holiness of God and the sinfulness of his human worshippers, that is about the great gulf that ever exists between the Lord and the people of earth. Further in the ministries of the priests and Levites concerning the sacrificial rites there are what are believed to be divinely-given opportunities for the securing forgiveness for certain of the sins of the people of God. Moreover, the gift of the sacrificial system that the Old Testament speaks about is used in certain parts of the New Testament to explain how the work of Christ is to be understood; in this regard see, for example, Heb 5:6, 10; 7:26–28; 9:13–14. Yet while Christians may in this way recall with thankfulness that for them the Old Testament's sacrificial rites have become outmoded, yet the historic reason for what was understood to be the gracious divine provision of them was the sheer ongoing and ever-present reality of the sinfulness of the people of earth. That deep awareness of human sinfulness is still there on the part of Christians today, and the whole matter is so eloquently expressed in the Psalter:

> Have mercy on me, O God,
>   according to your steadfast love;
> according to your abundant mercy
>   blot out my transgressions.

> Wash me thoroughly from my iniquity,
>   and cleanse me from my sin.
> For I know my transgressions,
>   and my sin is ever before me. (Ps 51:1–3)

And with such a human consciousness of sin before us we may recall one of the Old Testament's remarkable revelations concerning the mercy of God upon a sinner fleeing for his life, one whose bed was rough and ready in the open air but whose words of divine revelation to him suggest that place was indeed something of a "house of God."

> Then Jacob woke from his sleep and said, "Surely the LORD is in this place—and I did not know it!" And he was afraid, and said, "How awesome is this place! This is none other than the house of God, and this is the gate of heaven." (Gen 28:16–17)

So here is John of Damascus (c.675–c.749) many centuries later making reference in a Christian sermon to this passage; and the "you" he is speaking about is the Virgin Mary:

> I had nearly forgotten Jacob's ladder. Is it not evident to every one that it prefigured you, and is not the type easily recognized? Just as Jacob saw the ladder bringing together heaven and earth, and on it angels coming down and going up, and the truly strong and invulnerable God wrestling mystically with himself, so are you placed between us, and are become the ladder of God's descent towards us, of him who took upon himself our weakness, uniting us to himself, and enabling man to see God. You have brought together what was parted. Hence angels descended to him, ministering to him as their God and LORD, and men, adopting the life of angels, are carried up to heaven.

4

Life in Community

> For you are a people holy to the LORD your God;
> the LORD your God has chosen you out of all the peoples
> on earth to be his people, his treasured possession. (Deut 7:6)

THE VERSE QUOTED ABOVE, while its main emphasis may be on the fact that it is the Lord God who has chosen and called his people, also makes the point that it is a *whole* people who are called. That is, the emphasis here is upon the *community* rather than on various particular individuals. This is the subject of the present chapter, namely the people of Israel who are called to live as a community of people, something more than merely a collection of individuals.

We may begin with brief consideration of some words of just three of the Hebrew prophets, Isaiah of Jerusalem, Amos of Tekoa, and Micah of Moresheth. In the first place, Isaiah, in the opening chapter of the book that takes his name makes the point that that nation does consist of all the people, and that some individuals and groups have particular needs that the more fortunate among them are to remember in their lives:

> Wash yourselves; make yourselves clean;
>   remove the evil of your doings
>   from before my eyes;
> cease to do evil,
>   learn to do good;
> seek justice,
>   rescue the oppressed,
> defend the orphan,

plead for the widow. (Isa 1:16–17)

That is to say, the people of Israel make up a community, and further within that community there are individuals needing particular care, and concerning whom the more fortunate, and those called to offices and tasks in national and community life, should be aware, taking any necessary action.

Amos speaks not dissimilarly, but with the added emphasis on the matter and place of worship in the national life. Worship *should* have a central place in that life, but it must not be at the expense of lack of justice and righteousness towards those who at present are suffering and afflicted, nor take place as parts of the lives of those who do not live with cares and concerns for justice and righteousness. Thus the Lord says,

> I hate, I despise your festivals,
>   and I take no delight in your solemn assemblies.
> Even though you offer me your burnt offerings and grain offerings,
>   I will not accept them;
> and the offerings of well-being of your fatted animals
>   I will not look upon.
> Take away from me the noise of your songs;
>   I will not listen to the melody of your harps.
> But let justice roll down like waters,
>   and righteousness like an ever-flowing stream. (Amos 5:21–24)

And thirdly, what Micah has to say in this regard is along the same lines:

> He has told you, O mortal, what is good;
>   and what does the LORD require of you
> but to do justice, and to love kindness,
>   and to walk humbly with your God? (Mic 6:8)

That is to say, the members of this community, and in particular their leaders, are called upon to have a care that all members of that community are afforded full opportunities in the communal and national life. All are to be remembered and none is to be forgotten. Yet there is something else to be said—indeed emphasized—about this community life, namely, as we have already seen, its predominant focus, its orientation, is that it has a never-to-be-forgotten relationship, a covenant relationship, with its divine Lord, the Lord God of Israel. In the book of Exodus we have an account of the

covenant-making ceremony that follows on from the divine deliverance of
the people of Israel from Egypt, and in this we read:

> Now therefore, if you obey my voice and keep my covenant, you
> shall be my treasured possession out of all the peoples. Indeed,
> the whole earth is mine, but you shall be for me a priestly king-
> dom and a holy nation. (Exod 19:5–6)

In these two verses, the people of Israel's relationship with the Lord is
described in three phrases. First, we are told that subject to the limitation
and requirement that these people obey the Lord and keep his covenant
with them, they are to be the Lord's "treasured possession," and thus live as a
distinct and specially privileged people in the life of the world. Nevertheless,
as we read in various parts of the Old Testament this clearly did not mean
that they were in a state of immunity from the problems, the vicissitudes of
the sheer experience of living among the nations of the world in a series of
succeeding ages and eras. However, what it was that perhaps these people
of Israel were being given was help, believed to be divine help, in this living,
for they were in a special way the chosen people of the Lord, to whom they
could go in prayer, from whom they could seek guidance, and in whose
name they could receive strength for their ongoing journey of life, even deliverance in those situations beyond earthly change and redemption.

Then second, the people of Israel were told that they were destined
to be "a priestly kingdom," and here "priestly" would seem to be the crucial word. The Israelite priests were responsible for the religious life of the
people of Israel, in particular for teaching the people, for offering their sacrifices, indeed, for making sure those sacrifices and offerings were offered
in appropriate ways and at the appointed times so that the relationship with
the almighty and holy Lord was maintained. Surely the word "priestly" is
used here in the sense of what we might call "spiritual," that these people are
not portrayed as being just another of the nations on earth, but that there is
what we might call a *spiritual* dimension, a religious aspect, to who they are
and what they do.

The third expression used here is "a holy nation" that is to say the Israelites are to be "different" from other peoples, in that they have their particular relationship with the Lord. They are a people who are committed to
the Lord, thereby being different from others, and the fact that the word *holy*
is applied to them suggests that they both belong to God and are to live good
moral lives, indeed lives that are well-pleasing to God. As will emerge below
as this chapter develops, a serious emphasis in this covenant relationship is
a deep concern for the poor of the Israelite community, which already we

have seen in the above quotations from the prophecies of Isaiah, Amos, and Micah.

One commentator has said about the triad of statements concerning the Israelite people in Exod 19:5–6, "The covenant responsibility encompasses her whole life, defining her relation to God and to her neighbors, and the quality of her existence." Other parts of the Old Testament speak of the particular relationship between the nation and the Lord through the use of the word *love*. Thus, Hosea has "When Israel was a child, I loved him, and out of Egypt I called my son." (Hos 11:1; see also Isa 43:3–4; 48:14). Indeed, these are people who have, as it were, been specially chosen by God to be close to him. This matter also received some emphasis in the book of the prophet Ezekiel with its words "Thus says the LORD God: On the day when I chose Israel . . . I swore to them, saying, I am the LORD your God." (Ezek 20:5) Or we may observe that in Deut 10:15 this is expressed in the strongly worded formula, "the LORD set his heart in love on your ancestors alone and chose you, their descendants after them, out of all the peoples, as it is today." Walter Brueggemann speaks about this verse as contrasting the particularity of Israel over against the universal governance of Yahweh. Perhaps something of this emphasis on the special relationship between the Lord and Israel is reflected also in the somewhat enigmatic words of Num 23:9, "Here is a people living alone, and not reckoning itself among the nations!" One commentator has spoken of the emphasis here being on the special privilege of the Israelites among the surrounding nations. We may also note that there is a full account of a covenant-making ceremony in the book of Joshua (Josh 24:2–28), which goes into considerable detail in these matters of the relationship of the Lord with his people. Nor should texts such as Amos 3:2 with its "You only have I known of all the families of the earth", and "O send out your light and your truth; let them lead me" (Ps 43:3) be neglected in this regard, for again they both speak of the special and particular relationship the people of Israel corporately are to have with the Lord.

All this is to say that there is portrayed in parts of the Old Testament a close relationship between God and his people. In this covenant relationship not only is there to be exercised a particular care among the people for one another, and especially for those who in worldly terms are the least privileged, but also there is a quite special relationship portrayed in these documents between the Lord and his people, and which his people must ever remember. There is a spoken-about closeness between these parties, the divine and the human, a closeness that inevitably invokes a sense of human amazement and wonder. Further, in view of the fact that the divine part of the covenant parties has his dwelling in an extra-terrestrial setting, we may feel justified in making use of the word "spiritual" in our describing this divine-human relationship. This is different from the relationships between like-and-like in our inter-human relationships, distinct in that it is between parties who are not only so unlike, but also whose dwelling places are so dissimilar. We may perhaps, then, once again borrow the language of recent studies and writings on Christian divine—human relationships, and call this a *spiritual* relationship.

Clearly, both the maintenance and also the development of these relationships was not always easy, indeed at times laying considerable demands upon the people. In the book of Exodus—as we have earlier in this work observed—we read how on the holy mountain the Lord gave to Moses the "Ten Words"—what Christians call the Ten Commandments (Exod 20:1–17). These stress in the first place that there is a particular relationship between the Lord and his people, these being especially given to the people of Israel and not to others, namely, "I am the LORD your God, who brought you out of the land of Egypt, out of the house of slavery; you shall have no other gods before me." (Exod 20:2–3) Thus the Israelites are not to have idols of any type, nothing that may be worshipped apart from their Lord, and nor are they to make wrongful or disrespectful use of the name of the Lord; let it be, rather, that the mere mention of the Lord's name does invoke within these people a due sense of awe, praise, and deep dependence (Exod 20:4–7). These commandments then go on to other matters that are to have high priority in the lives of the Israelite people, these being set out in Exod 20:8–17. The first issue dealt with here, and this in considerable detail, is instructions about the seventh day of the week, the sabbath day (vv. 8–11), and the emphasis is on this as a day of rest for all people, for all the members of a family, including slaves, livestock and the resident aliens in the towns. There is nothing here about worship being commanded to take place on the Sabbath—rather this is intended to be a day of rest for all. Then follow the commands to honor parents, not to commit murder, nor to commit adultery, nor to steal, nor to bear false witness against neighbors (vv. 12–16). Finally comes the detailed commandment that there is to be no coveting of one's neighbor's house—or indeed of anything else that belongs to the neighbor (v. 17).

The Ten Commandments are presented in rather different form in the book of Deuteronomy, here set forth as having been given by the Lord to his people during the course of their journey from Horeb to the promised land (Deut 5:1–33). These do not call to be considered in detail in this work, but what we do need to take note of is that in other parts of the Old Testament there are further and detailed instructions about how life is to be lived by God's people in the world. An extensive piece of such writing is that block of material in the book of Leviticus chs 17 to 26, generally known as the Holiness Code. This is so-named because in its extensive teaching we have the divine word that as God is holy (separate, awesome), so also are his people to be holy—different from other nations in their attitudes to one another and to others, and to their Lord—in both their individual and their corporate lives in the world. Thus here are outlined matters about blood (ch 17); about forbidden sexual relationships (ch 18); much detail about being holy, including care for those in the Israelite community who are poor, or are migrants, or who have more generally fallen on difficult times (chs 19–20); detailed laws for those who are called to be priests (ch 21); laws about various matters including offering sacrifices (ch 22); a good deal about festivals (ch 23); about lamps in the sanctuary, the bread of the presence, and questions about blasphemy; sabbatical and jubilee years, not forgetting blessings and curses (chs 24–26). These detailed matters do not need to detain us at this present time, but we shall later return to them in a consideration of how they are to be understood—and acted upon or not—by Christians in our contemporary world. See further, below, ch 7.

In the meantime we can appreciate that in the Old Testament we are given a real sense of the Israelites being portrayed as a people who are intended by the Lord to be different from the peoples of other nations; the people of Israel are to have standards and morals not necessarily shared by other nations; they are a people called to live in community, and further have—and are called to maintain faithfully—a particular and special relationship with the Lord God.

But, we may ask, how will this precious, life-giving, divinely instituted covenant relationship be maintained by the Israelites, as they have inevitably to live in the world in the midst of various other nations? For the witness of both human experience, and also of what we read in the pages of the Old Testament, strongly suggest that there will be constant temptations to go in other ways, both other religious ways and also in other worldly ways. Perhaps it was for this reason that there arose, or there developed in the Israelite society—or we might wish to say there were divinely given—a number of appointments and callings intended to be for the maintenance and the strengthening of the covenant relationship. We can understand such appointments as divine gifts given to these people to assist them in their being the holy God's own holy people (Lev 19:2–3). Thus we shall now consider some of those who were appointed to such callings in the life of God's people, as they sought as a nation amidst other nations and traditions of belief and worship, to live in faithful covenant relationship with its Lord God.

Priests and Levites

The calling of the Old Testament priesthood was in the first place into the ministry of offering gifts and sacrifices at the altar, that is carrying out the rituals we considered in the preceding chapter whereby it was believed sins were forgiven, and fellowship between God and his people was restored. In particular it was concern with the *blood* of the sacrifice that was the special priestly responsibility, for as we have already seen there was something crucial in the blood—it was through the blood that atonement was made, that there was brought about the renewed "at-one-ment" between the divine and human parties. See further above, ch 3. The priests were also responsible for the use of incense in worship, for leading the people in prayer, and for teaching them about religious matters.

It is difficult to be precise about the role of the Levites in these ministries, for their responsibilities seem to have changed over the course of time, and we are not given sufficient information to be clear just how, or when, they changed. We might say in the most general terms that the Levites were called to assist the priests in their priestly ministry, but at the same time to observe that there was one particular responsibility, at least at one particular historical moment, that fell to them. This we have already observed in the preceding chapter, the ministry of helping the people understand the law that was being read to them in a solemn day in Jerusalem in the days of Ezra and Nehemiah.

In these ways the priests and Levites exercised their ministries in the covenant relationship of their people with the Lord. Clearly they had a crucial role to fulfill: they were responsible for helping an ever-sinful people to live in on-going fellowship with a holy God, which is to say that they were involved in particular ways with *spiritual* matters, and with the *spirituality* of their peoples' relationship with the Lord. Truly, the successful continuance and maintenance of the covenant was dependent upon what the priests and the Levites were called to be and to do. We should surely see the priestly and levitical ministries as divine gifts given, it was believed, by the Lord of the covenant to his people of earth, to assist them in the keeping of that covenant relationship.

Kings

The kings of Israel and Judah, it has to be said, receive a very mixed, in fact largely negative, assessment in the Old Testament. Remarkably few of them were given positive assessments in those characteristic summary statements at the close of the account of each reign in the books of Kings. See, for example, 2 Kgs 13:10–13 for the brief and not uncritical account of the reign of Jehoash over the northern kingdom of Israel.

In early times when the Israelite tribes moved into Canaan we read that they appointed those who were called Judges in periods of crisis when they needed to defend themselves against enemies, each Judge being appointed just for the period of that emergency. This phase of Israel's life, those times in which these Judges judged, we can read about in the Old Testament book of Judges.

However, when we turn to the first book of Samuel we are reading about the perceived need on the part of some of the people of Israel that they, like the nations round about them, should have a king. Yet at the same time there were those who saw the dangers of such a move, who could see certain warning signals in the appointment for life of a person with kingly powers. No doubt these stories in the early chapters of the Samuel books reflect later debates, controversies that came out of the sheer experience of having kings who in the nature of kingship would have great power and authority in their realms. The experience of Israelite kingship was indeed in general a mixed one: truly some kings did rule their people with justice and righteousness, but others, perhaps inevitably, succumbed to some degree or other to the temptations of power or wealth, or both, to what would later come to be so famously expressed by Lord Acton (1834–1902) in a letter to Bishop Mandell Creighton, "Power tends to corrupt and absolute power corrupts absolutely."

And alas, so it was for the people of Israel. King David had remarkable military successes, and was able to pass on a united kingdom to his son and successor Solomon. Amongst other places David had captured Jerusalem, making it his own city, the city that the line of David would be able to pass on through the generations of his own family. Yet while David may have gained for his people so much, he at the same time was able to use his authority and power for his own purposes, such as being able to have for his own wife Bathsheba who was already married to Uriah the Hittite. Not that David's son and successor, Solomon, was any better. While on the one hand Solomon continued the work of David in enhancing the city of Jerusalem, building a temple for the purposes of public, indeed national, worship and the seeking of the Lord, he also built a great royal palace for himself and his successors—and we cannot help but take notice of the fact that according to the records we have, the royal palace was larger than the divine temple (compare 1 Kgs 6:2 with 7:1–8)! So also, we read of Solomon making use of his royal powers to acquire for himself many wives, never mind all those horses we are told he had, along with so much else as we can read in 1 Kgs

10:1–29. Manifestly, there are aspects of the life and work of these kings that were hardly in tune with the spiritual nature of their being called by the Lord to such high responsibilities.

For while the kings were appointed to protect their people from any warlike aspirations on the part of their neighbors, they were also expected to safeguard the rights and possessions of the less wealthy in their own lands, in particular those of the poor. One of the Old Testament's classic cases of this *not* happening was, as we saw above in ch 2 (see above, pp.46–47), the acquisition of the vineyard that bordered on one of the king's palaces which was owned by a certain Naboth, in fact to whose family the vineyard had belonged for generations. For another example we can read of a king being challenged by a prophet, we may turn to the book of Amos, where we read of this prophet preaching in the northern kingdom of Israel. Clearly the authorities loyal to the king in the northern kingdom of Israel did not approve at all of the preaching of Amos, in particular that he was declaiming against the king and his exercise of his powers. Amos spoke of the Lord setting a plumb line in the midst of the people of Israel. Thus was the priest of Bethel to send this troublesome prophet on his way, in particular to go back to his own land of Judah and prophesy there, but definitely not in Israel. See Amos 7:10–17.

All this is to say that the Israelite king while he may have occupied a very privileged place in Israelite society, was called to protect the rights of his people, and especially the rights of those who were powerless and unable to help themselves. These matters are set forth in a series of biblical Psalms concerned with the privileges and duties of the Israelite king, and which, as we have seen, have been called Royal Psalms. Psalm 2 is the first of these, and it stresses the high place accorded to the king, here going as far as saying that he is none other than the Lord's son (Ps 2:7). Therefore let other kings on earth take note, and respect him, indeed, serve him (vv. 10–11). That the king can here be referred to as being none other than the Lord's son makes it clear that what is being spoken about is the king's spiritual relationship with the Lord. From a purely earthly point of view, the king would have been the son of a man, most likely himself a king. Yet, such kingly men are portrayed in Ps 2 as having at the same time a particular and spiritual relationship with the Lord. This is nothing less than the Lord's king who has been divinely set on Zion, on the Lord's "holy hill" (Ps 2:6). Further, we are told, and now it is the king who is speaking,

> I will tell of the decree of the LORD:
> He said to me, "You are my son;
> today I have begotten you . . ." (Ps 2:7)

Another of the Royal Psalms that calls for comment is Ps 72, which first offers a prayer that the king may be given a true sense of justice, may there be prosperity in the land, and may the king defend the rights of the poor of the people (vv. 1–4). These and other matters are set forth in the following verses, now with more detail: may he have a long and caring reign (vv. 5–7; 16–17); may he receive worldwide tributes, his own lands not being threatened by other kings and nations (vv. 8–11, 15); may he in his own land deliver the poor and needy (vv. 12–14). For such indeed were some of the important duties and cares of the Israelite kings, as they, each in their own generation, used their highest of offices to protect their covenant people from external forces, and to ensure that the poor and powerless at home be given all due care and attention. For thus the kings of Israel and Judah, along with the priests and the Levites, were entrusted with particular duties in the maintenance of the divinely instituted covenant relationship of the Lord God with his chosen people. Yet there is a third group of people, it was believed sent by the Lord, who would assist the peoples in this covenant maintenance, and these were the prophets and to a brief consideration of their ministries in this regard we now turn.

Prophets

The Hebrew prophets are portrayed as having been called individually by the Lord to give voice to the Lord's will and purposes for his people. That is, as a part of their divine call, they had specific and vital matters to convey to the nation for some particular historical moment, or moments. One of the great insights they brought to their peoples was that those people needed to see, understand, and take notice of the fact that a number of other nations were around Israel and Judah, and that in worldly terms those foreign nations would then, and on into the future, inevitably bring about changes in the lives of the peoples of Israel and Judah. Indeed we may say that the Old Testament prophets were called to help their peoples see and understand that they were in a world where there were other nations, some of them very large and powerful, and further that the people of Israel were in a world that was changing—in no small way because of the needs and ambitions of these larger nations. In fact, we could say that these prophets had been called by God to help their peoples see anew their own place among the nations, and to understand that place not only in geographical dimensions, but also in historical terms, and even further in spiritual contexts. For the prophets are portrayed in the Old Testament as having been called to help their peoples see the spiritual and other dimensions and aspects of life in the world. For gone now were the days when under the rule of a King David, or even of a King Solomon, they were able to have a prominent place among the nations. Now there were other strong, powerful nations who fundamentally and in worldly terms would be "calling the tune" of life.

In the cases of some of these Hebrew prophets, we read about what appear to have been a number of remarkable divine, spiritual experiences of and with the Lord, out of which there seem to have come calls from God to proclaim to their people divine words and concerns. Sometimes the story of this experience of the Lord and of his call to an individual is told in considerable fullness as in the case, for example, of Isaiah (see Isa 6:1–13). In other cases the call account raises the note of protest on the part of the one who was called, such as we read about with Jeremiah (Jer 1:4–19). Or it might come to such a one as Amos who appears to have been well-occupied in his life with husbandry and herds (Amos 7:14). What is portrayed as changing so dramatically when these people were called by the Lord was that there appears to have been added into their lives a deep consciousness of the fact that they had been called into a deep and quite special relationship with the Lord, and to the addition into their lives of an ongoing closeness in relationship with the Lord, in fact to the entering into what we might call the spiritual realm. Thus were particular divine expectations, wills, judgments given to them for proclamation to their peoples, intended for that particular day and age. Those divine words and concerns were with both individual and personal religious matters, and also with great and large concerns about their peoples' place in what were a series of growing dramas and times of great changes, even upheavals, sometimes developments in the world in which they were now but just a very small part. That is to say, the prophets were concerned to proclaim something of these matters to their peoples, to assist them with the matter of change in the world around them, and thus enable them in a succession of new ages to continue to live in the terms and ongoing reality of the ancient covenant relationship. For our present purposes something of this may be illustrated by considering a number of examples drawn from the books of the prophets and from books that give stories about the activities of some of the Lord's prophets.

One of the themes that regularly appears in the Old Testament books of the prophets is of the call to ensure that among God's people there was justice, in particular that those who were without wealth and authority did not suffer by failing to receive their fair share of what was available. Thus we find in the vision of the of a future leader spoken about by Isaiah,

> For a child has been born for us,
> a son given to us;

authority rests upon his shoulders;
and he is named
Wonderful Counselor, Mighty God,
  Everlasting Father, Prince of Peace.
His authority shall grow continually,
  and there shall be endless peace
for the throne of David and his kingdom.
  He will establish and uphold it
with justice and with righteousness
  from this time onward and forevermore.
The zeal of the LORD of hosts will do this. (Isa 9:6–7)

That is to say, all parts of the Israelite society, from the wealthiest to the poorest, from the most fortunate to the least fortunate, all were to be included in that covenant relationship of God and his people. Indeed, all these peoples were believed to be in that spiritual relationship of God and his people we have considered, and that those who were wealthy in worldly terms were called to be sharers of something of their wealth with those who were poor, defenseless, or on their own. This, we have seen, is there right at the beginning of the Isaiah book, and we find it again, expressed in remarkably forthright terms in the book of the prophet Amos (see Amos 5:18–24; 7:14–17), and memorably in Micah (Mic 6:8).

Another ministry of the Hebrew prophets was to help their peoples understand something about the clashes of the nations around them in the terms of a total world situation that was the Lord Yahweh's world; that is to see the life of the whole world as being ultimately, mysteriously under the rule of the Lord and within the whole purview of the divine purposes. For example, two chapters of the book of Isaiah are devoted to detailed accounts of happenings in Judah and Jerusalem when they were besieged by a coalition of the kings of Israel and Syria (the so-called Syro-Ephraimite war—see Isa chs 7 and 8). What we are told the prophet Isaiah was called to say about this is framed by an opening narrative in visionary language and concepts speaking of his call to prophetic servanthood in that experience of the Lord's appearance to him in the temple (Isa 6:1–13), and is completed by the promise of the coming one day of the ideal earthly king both to govern and also to care for his people with divine authority, be a father to them, and to bring them peace (Isa 9:2–7). That is, the life of two earthly kingdoms with all their earthiness is brought into a much greater setting, that of the rule of the Lord, and of the ongoing purposes of God. The prophet here is portrayed as seeking to help his people understand their local and national comings and goings as being a part of the ongoing life of the world that is so mysteriously governed by the Lord God. This means that what may appear at one level to be merely worldly and human-led happenings, is appreciated at a deeper and spiritual level as being caught up in the divine purposes. That is to say, the ministry of the Hebrew prophet included, among other things, what we might refer to as a certain drawing together of the life of heaven and the life of the world. Thus there was something quite specifically *spiritual* about the ministry and the message of the prophet given by the Lord God, that was to be proclaimed to the Lord's people on earth. We are given similar visions through the insertions into the records of the prophetic words of Amos to his peoples: a series of doxologies in which the Lord is exalted and praised in fulsome words as lord and creator (Amos 4:13; 5:8–9; 9:5–6).

Some of the Old Testament prophets are portrayed as praying for their people, and in this were engaged in a further task in helping their people be a more faithful community of the Lord, surely a *spiritual* ministry if there ever was one. So we read of Amos praying for his people, in particular that their sins may be forgiven (Amos 7:2–3, 5–6), of Hosea giving his people a prayer for them to use as they turn to the Lord (Hos 14:2–3), of Jeremiah praying at one time for his people (Jer 14:21; 18:20), though not at another time—because the people were so very deep in their sins, perhaps beyond being prayed for? (Jer 7:16; 11:14; 14:11, 13; 15:1) Nor should we forget that in earlier times we are told that Moses prayed for the people (Exod 32:11–14, 30–34), as also would Samuel (1 Sam 12:17–23), and thus further this would be a concern of one of the "Servant" passages in Isaiah 40–55, where the Lord's servant is portrayed as, among other things, remembering his people in prayer (Isa 52:13—53:12, esp. 53:12).

Sages

There is a distinctive group of writings in the Old Testament that have a number of intellectual characteristics, in particular there being within them a sense of profound grappling with some aspects of the religious beliefs of the people of Israel. That is, there is in these writings the attempt to give some sort of theological explanation, for example, for the occurrence, the experience, and the problem of suffering. For if God is the God who cares for his people, and who is renowned for his deliverance of them from their times of suffering and constriction in their lives, why is it that religious people in age after age continue to experience sufferings and setbacks? These issues are real and mysterious at all times for those of faith, and the Old Testament has a significant number of documents that deal in one way or another with them. To these matters we shall return in ch 6 below, in the chapter entitled "Life with Questions," but in the meantime we should take note of the fact that in the Hebrew Bible there are references to certain servants of the Lord for whom modern scholarship has given the general title "Sages," that is "Wise people," those whose ministries are written about in the so-called "Wisdom Writings," writings intended to give help, guidance, inspiration for people in their sufferings and times of religious difficulty and even, at times, confusion. Such contributions are what we know as the books of Proverbs, Job, and Ecclesiastes, but further the issues dealt with in them are to be found elsewhere, for example among the psalms and in various other places in the Old Testament. It is more than understandable that thinking people of Old Testament times needed help and encouragement for their times of suffering, and we may thus see these so-called wisdom writers, these Sages as having been given, along with priests and Levites, kings and prophets, as servants of the Lord to assist God's people to live in hope, faith, and faithfulness their covenant relationship with the Lord. Yet this is a large subject that warrants a chapter of its own in this work, and therefore is a matter to which we shall return. See below ch 6.

From Texts to Spirituality

Here we once again consider the question, "What do the Old Testament passages we have considered in this chapter contribute to a Christian spirituality in the present-day world?" In particular what is there in these texts that we do not find in the New Testament, and which thus for their particular emphases and insights we are somewhat the more dependent upon the Old Testament? It certainly would seem that among the matters we have considered that the Old Testament sets before us about living in community, are considerable challenges to some of us in the contemporary western world where there is a pronounced tendency to emphasize the life of the individual rather than that of the community. There is a further challenge here for us in that we are called to be a holy people of a holy Lord, and it is surely all too easy to forget about this distinctive call to be different, to have particular standards, to have a concern for all of our contemporary neighbors—both those who are near and those who geographically are far away. What then, can we say by way of summary about the Old Testament's guidance for us about our life, and our lives in community.

The call surely comes clearly to us through the witness of the Old Testament that we are to have a real concern for the poor and those who have insufficient to maintain viable life without outside help. Where the Old Testament reads "orphans, widows" should there not be an application in the western world in the twenty-first century to those who have been called "migrants" and "refugees"? In fact, as we have seen above one of the great ministries of the Old Testament prophets was to understand, and therefore to proclaim, that there is a certain relationship, even "closeness" between heaven and earth, between God and his people in the various parts of earth, out of which comes a certain call to us to consider the life of the world and its people not merely in human and conventional political terms but the more as all of us are envisaged as being involved in the purposes of God. Further, in the contemporary world is there not a real and continuing need for the present-day successors of the kings of old, those who will direct the affairs of our states in justice and righteousness, that they will have a care for all, especially those who have such small voices? Do we not continue to need urgently those who will seek for us the forgiveness of our sins and teach us about the things of life that are beyond mere getting and gaining; for those who will help us to deal with our tragedies and setbacks? Do we not need in all ages, and for all who are either wealthy in worldly terms or else poor in those things, a deep and ongoing sense and challenge that we are called to be the holy people of the holy God, because ever and always there will surely be those who will need help and assistance in the living of their lives in the world? Is there not a deep continuing need in the contemporary world for people with influence, power and responsibility not to use such gifts as they have been given for their personal enrichment and self-aggrandizement, but who will seek the good of all, in particular having a care for those who have little both in goods and also in power? Is there not above all a continued need of those who will seek to live holy lives and who will remain humble pilgrims with the Lord? And do we not ever need those humble ones in the communities of faith, those who will indeed do justice and who will love mercy?

John Calvin in one of his lectures in Geneva, when he came to speak about Mic 6:8 ("He has told you, O mortal, what is good; and what does the Lord require of you but to do justice, and to love kindness, and to walk humbly with your God?") said,

> The Prophet, therefore, mentions justice and mercy, not that God casts aside that which is principal—the worship of his name; but he shows, by evidences or effects, what true religion is.
>
> Hypocrites place all holiness in external rites; but God requires what is very different; for his worship is spiritual. But as hypocrites can make a show of great zeal and of great solicitude in the outward worship of God, the Prophets try the conduct of men in another way, by inquiring whether they act justly and

kindly towards one another, whether they are free from all fraud and violence, whether they observe justice and show mercy.

Further, in more recent times Thomas Merton observed,

Our nature, which is a free gift of God, was given to us to be perfected and enhanced by another free gift that is not due it. . . . . This free gift is "sanctifying grace." It perfects our nature with the gift of a life, an intellection, a love, a mode of existence infinitely above its own level.

5

Life in a Changing World

> When the house of David heard that Aram had allied itself with
> Ephraim, the heart of Ahaz and the heart of his people shook as
> the trees of the forest shake before the wind. (Isa 7:2)

"The lamentable change is from the best" as Edgar observes in Act IV
of Shakespeare's play *King Lear*, and all too often changes in life appear to us
rather like that, not so much for the better, but rather for the worse. The Old
Testament in its various documents certainly has a good deal of transition
to record and speak about, and sometimes those transitions are for the good
and at times for the less good. This present chapter is concerned with some
of the major changes that the people of Old Testament times experienced,
and what were some of the aspects of those alterations in their national
circumstances that affected the people of Israel. In this modest study I am
making the assumption that what the Old Testament has to say about matters historical is to be accepted as such. Even so, it does have to be said that
for many years scholarly questions have been raised about the historical ac-
curacy of parts of the Old Testament, documents that are clearly in the first
place concerned with theological matters. Yet for us all, development of our
theological viewpoints, and thus of our spirituality, can surely be brought
about through worldly changes in our situations and circumstances.

"The house of David" referred to in the above quotation is King Ahaz
who reigned in Judah and Jerusalem in a period of the eighth century BCE,
whose father and grandfather had been Judean kings, namely Kings Jothan
and Uzziah. As we saw in ch 4 above, pp.80–81 this was the crisis of the
so-called Syro-Ephraimite war, that we are told caused hearts of king and

people to shake like wind-swept trees. In this situation the prophet Isaiah sought to assure king Ahaz, the people of Judah, and the residents and officials in Jerusalem that they had little to fear, for this coalition was made up of "two smouldering stumps of firebrands" (Isa 7:4).

And indeed, the people of Israel had known worse situations, and in later times would certainly come to experience far greater crises. For surely the fact is that all peoples wish to have a share in the lands of the world so that they may live in quietness and peace, and yet inevitably the possession of certain parts of the land will attract other leaders and peoples of nations who are seeking land and space for themselves. How very precious to all peoples are their lands—land in which they may live in peace; land on which their food may be grown; land where their homes may be established and be passed on to future generations. Already, within the first book of the Old Testament after a reasonably peaceful start in this regard we are told of a situation of starvation in the land of Israel which leads to the brothers of Joseph going to Egypt to seek there for food. By a seemingly mysterious series of human events, indeed by what come to be seen and understood as divine provisions and providences, this leads them to find in Egypt not only their brother Joseph, now in high office in the service of the Egyptian Pharaoh, but also more than adequate provisions of food for all their family needs. See Gen 42:1—50:26. Thus do the Israelites, or at least some of them, come to take up residence in the land of Egypt, and live in peace and plenty.

Still, that does not last forever, and by the beginning of the book of Exodus we learn that the time came when a later Pharaoh assumed power in Egypt, a Pharaoh who did not know Joseph (Exod 1:8), which is to say that there was no longer a comfortable and close relationship between the Egyptian ruler and the Israelite Joseph and his family and successors. Thus it was, so we read in the book of Exodus, that Moses was called to be the leader of the Lord's people, and this he eventually did, being enabled to bring his people to the very verge of the promised land of Canaan, including what is portrayed as an extended halt where much happened at the foot of what is called in our records Mount Sinai/Horeb. This extended stay at the foot of the holy mountain is where the writers of the book of Exodus portray so much of the sacred covenant relationship between God and the Israelites being made. Here are given many details as to ways of earthly life to be adopted in family and other human relationships with the Lord God. There are many details too about places of worship, one in particular that looks very suitable for life in the desert, and another that is so elaborate and costly that—as we have already observed—must surely be what many years later came to be built in the Israelites' capital city of Jerusalem.

Enough has been said to make the point with which we are particu-larly concerned in this present chapter, namely that the people of God, as they are portrayed in the Old Testament, are a people called to live out their religious lives—their spiritual lives—in the world. That is, in the world that is a both a changing world, even an ever-changing world, and a world being earnestly sought that can afford to leaders and people an ongoing sense of peace and security, and which at other times cannot.

Thus while we are given accounts of the Lord's provision for the Isra-elites of adequate quantities of food and drink for the desert journey (see for example Exod 16:1—17:16), there is at the end of that journey the great challenge of finding a place for themselves in the land to which they have travelled, and which is already seemingly well-occupied by established groups and people. The Israelites' progress into their "promised land" is in the Old Testament portrayed as being greatly, indeed divinely, assisted by none other than their Lord God (see for example Josh 6:1–27). This does inevitably constitute something of a problem for Christian readers of these documents with its talk of driving out these occupying nations both through their own military prowess but also with the assistance, the back-ing, the guidance of none other than the Lord God. The ethics of driving out other peoples so that the aggressors can find, appropriate, and occupy lands, towns, villages is undoubtedly one of the problematic parts of the Old Testament for Christian readers of it today, and this whole matter is given some attention in ch 7 below on the subject of "Life with Ethical Concerns."

Still there was far more of this to come, yet also with something of tables being turned for the people of Israel in that they became defenders of what they had gained by way of lands and possessions in their promised land of Canaan. Thus in the book of Judges we read of the appointment of a succession of judges, those who appear to have been called in the various times of crisis to rescue their peoples from the advances and encroachments of other nations. But then came the call that they should have a more per-manent type of national leadership, like a king to be their defender. Judging from what we read in the first book of Samuel there seems to have been a lively debate for and against having kings—for while an individual with the power and authority of a king might defend the people from their enemies, equally such a ruler might take personal advantage of the power, privileges, even perhaps wealth, that would come with their office and responsibili-ties. At any rate the people of Israel did decide to have a king, and thus Saul became the first king in Israel, but clearly he had mixed fortunes and successes in the office. He was followed by David, the son of Jesse, who certainly was very gifted in leadership, and was able to expand and protect the nation's borders. Above all David captured the city of Jerusalem, making it his capital city, and withal a most worthy place to serve as the center of the Israelite nation. Yet, there were clear overreaching and personal privileges for David, so that there was an attempted, yet unsuccessful, *coup d'état* which we read about in 2 Sam 20:1–26.

With the death of David, Solomon came into his kingship, and with him the addition of a great temple in Jerusalem, and also the great royal palace, much of the work being carried out on these large projects with foreign help, supplies, and labor. Here was a new aspect of Israel coming into the life and the world of the nations, for we read of the visit of the Queen of Sheba to see for herself what she had heard so much about (1 Kgs 10:1–13). But clearly all was not well for all the people of Israel as far as the kingship was concerned, for on the death of Solomon there was a real division of the kingdom. While the tribe of Judah and the city of David remained faithful to the dynasty of David, the more northerly tribes became independent and chose their own king, at first Jeroboam the son of Nebat (1 Kgs 11:26—14:20), and for the most part in the following years choosing a variety of different people to be their leaders, very few of them in dynastic succession with those who went before them. Nevertheless, thus politically did the Israelites continue until the northern kingdom of Israel was overrun by the Assyrians in 722 BCE and later the southern kingdom of Judah by the Babylonians in 587 BCE. Yet, throughout all this period of Israelite history, there was the ever-present problem that while on the one hand these peoples needed the institution of kingship for national good and protection, yet there was the other ever-present problem of the kings using their powers to make good and often more-than-adequate provision purely for themselves.

This somewhat lengthy digression into these historical details of the kingdoms of Israel and Judah has been necessary in order to provide some background understanding regarding certain of the future happenings and changes that would occur for the kingdoms of Israel and Judah, as they took their places among the other kingdoms, both great and small, in that part of the world. As already indicated at the beginning of this present chapter, a comparatively early happening, occurring in about the year 734 BCE, was that the kingdom of Israel (Ephraim) joined with the kingdom of Aram (Syria) and laid siege to Judah and Jerusalem, hoping to put their own nominee on the Jerusalem throne. This, the so-called Syro-Ephraimite war, is spoken about in Isa 7:1—8:22; 2 Kgs 16:1–20; 2 Chr 28:1–27; and very likely also in Hos 5:8—7:16.

It is clear from what we read in the book of Isaiah that there was a serious degree of panic felt in Jerusalem at this attack upon them, for we read that Ahaz's heart and the heart of his people shook as the trees of the forest shake before the wind (Isa 7:2). The words of Isaiah suggest that the prophet thought that this fear was unnecessary, and that king and people should stand firm in faith, "If you do not stand firm in faith, you shall not stand at all" (Isa 7:9), for the reason that the attacking forces of Israel and Aram were but "two smoldering stumps of firebrands" (Isa 7:4). This, however did not calm the troubled heart of king Ahaz, for according to the account in the books of Kings he appealed to Tiglath-pileser the king of Assyria saying, "I am your servant and your son. Come up, and rescue me from the hand of the king of Aram and from the hand of the king of Israel, who are attacking me." (2 Kgs 16:7)

Now, according to the books of Kings, Ahaz had already committed grievous sins in adopting worship practices of the nations round about, in particular engaging in child sacrifice, and making sacrifices and offerings on high places, on the hills, and under green trees—that is engaging in the worship practices of the Canaanites, all matters that for the Old Testament authors were totally unacceptable (2 Kgs 16:1–4). That is to say, what we are reading about here is a Judean king who in the eyes of authors of the Old Testament documents was already engaged in some unacceptable worship practices of the surrounding peoples, and who also went to plead for help in his military difficulties to a foreign king of a neighboring mighty country, namely Assyria. Thus were Israel and Judah becoming involved in the lives and fortunes of the nations round about them. While for the Old Testament getting involved in foreign worship practices was anathema, yet at the same time it must have been inevitable that in other ways Israel and Judah would have become involved in international matters, for no doubt one rather uncomfortable fact was that geographically they were in the area between the empires of Egypt and Mesopotamia, which is to say that they were in the nature of "buffer states" between the great powers of the day. Each of the powers as and when they could would have liked to have exercised control of these small states!

This was indeed a period of growing international and neighboring powers as far as the people of Israel were concerned. In those earlier times of the kingships of Saul, David and Solomon, the states of Israel, and later of Israel and Judah, had been able to have their ambitions and excursions into expanding their territories and gaining certain glories, but with the growth of the neighboring and far greater powers what was in the past was indeed gone.

Further, for the people of Israel and Judah this period was the age of what have been called the great prophets, that is the prophets whose words and teachings have come to be recorded and that we have in their resultant forms in the Old Testament, namely Isaiah, Jeremiah, Ezekiel, and the Twelve, the twelve so-called minor prophets. Now a number of the Old

Testament books of these prophets have blocks of materials which scholarship has called "Oracles against the nations" (see Amos 1:3—2:3; Isa 13–23; Jer 46–51; Ezek 25–32), in which the prophets range round the neighboring nations, criticizing them for their sins and failures. For indeed the fact is that in this period we are considering there was the experience for the people of Israel and Judah of a whole new age of living among a number of other and much larger nations. No longer were Israel and Judah able to enjoy independence in their comparatively small and compact lands centered on Jerusalem and Samaria, and other such places as, for example, Tekoa and Bethlehem, Megiddo and Dan and elsewhere, being able to live in a fairly high degree of freedom and independence. For surrounding these little states of Judah and Israel—and indeed at certain times dominating them—was arising in power a succession of nations and powers; Egypt and Assyria, then later Babylonia, followed historically by the Persian, then the Greek, and eventually the Roman empires.

What did this whole change in their situations mean for the leaders and peoples of Israel and Judah now they had what can only be called overlords, leaders of other nations, no doubt of other religious persuasions, that is those in power over them who had their own particular priorities? On the positive side the Israelites and Judeans had a certain protection from enemies and other outside military forces, but no doubt the little states of the likes of Israel and Judah had to pay taxes to gain that. Thus, when in military danger they no doubt had the assurance of more-than adequate help and strength. But then, what might the *religious* consequences of that military help have been? We do not hear in the Old Testament of either Israelite or Judean rulers having to adopt certain religious ways and stances that were not acceptably Yahwistic for their own religious leaders. Yet on the other hand we do read, for example, of King Ahaz of Judah when he came back from meeting the Assyrian ruler Tiglath-pileser in Damascus wished to have in the Jerusalem temple an altar like the one he had seen in Damascus (2 Kgs 16:10–11). We are not told whether this was a matter of having to do this on the orders or instructions of the authorities in Damascus or of the Assyrian ruler, Tiglath-pileser, or whether rather it was an altar that Ahaz simply liked the look of, and that therefore he wished to have one like that himself to be placed and thus serve in his own temple in Jerusalem. Or then, did Ahaz perhaps wish to ingratiate himself with his new overlord and so took for his own temple one of the "Assyrian style" altars?

Yet perhaps this comparatively small incident is sufficient to highlight what was for some of the writers whose work has gone into the Old Testament the danger for the Israelite people of adopting certain of the religious ways and ceremonies of neighboring nations. There was thus the serious possibility of the faith of the people of Judah and Israel suffering contamination, or even of having inappropriate additions made to it. This is a particular concern we find expressed in the book of Deuteronomy, namely that the people of Israel are called to be "a people holy to the Lord your God; the Lord your God has chosen you out of all the peoples on earth to be his people, his treasured possession." (Deut 7:6) Further, Deuteronomy has a deep-seated concern that this faith will become contaminated through contact in a particular way with the Canaanites, and thus it lays down strict instructions:

> If anyone secretly entices you . . . saying, "Let us go and worship other gods," whom neither you nor your ancestors have known, any of the gods of the peoples that are around you . . . you must not yield to or heed any such persons. (Deut 13:6–8)

Clearly this deuteronomic point of view is given much emphasis in the Old Testament's Books of Samuel and Kings, which thus have been called the "Deuteronomistic History." In fact all the kings of the northern kingdom of Israel, and almost all those of the southern kingdom of Judah are condemned for their having allowed such things to take place in their realms during their kingships. This is to be observed, for example, in what is said in the account of the reign of Ahaz of Judah with its words of condemnation,

> He even made his son pass through fire, according to the abominable practices of the nations whom the LORD drove out before the people of Israel. He sacrificed and made offerings on the high places, on the hills, and under every green tree. (2 Kgs 16:3–4)

There is some more history to be considered briefly, and then we can make some general comments about what all this perhaps suggests for those who turn to the Old Testament documents in their search for any guidance it may have for their Christian spirituality. However, first it needs to be said that in about the year 722 BCE the northern kingdom of Israel suffered considerable defeat at the hands of the Assyrian forces, and that its leaders and some of its peoples were taken away into exile, we are told to Halar, on the Habor, the river of Gozan, and in the cities of the Medes (see 2 Kgs 17:5–6). And that, it has to be said, is the last that we hear in the Old Testament about the northern Israelite tribes, they becoming what are sometimes referred to as the ten lost tribes of Israel, having spawned somewhat inevitably a whole series of theories about what possibly happened to them. As far as the Old Testament is concerned its silence over these tribes of the old northern kingdom of Israel is, we have to assume, due to the fact that henceforward the historical records and the religious writings from Israelite sources would come from scribes and other leaders in Jerusalem in the southern kingdom of Judah. At the same time the whole incident of the disappearance of these northern tribes from both the land of Israel and also from the pages of the Old Testament is a somewhat salutary comment on the potential dangers for some comparatively small groups of people and nations in eras of great and powerful kingdoms. This would be particularly so if the ruling nation considered that the subject peoples were being troublesome or difficult.

The southern kingdom of Judah with its capital city of Jerusalem had well over a hundred years still to go in its own land, being ruled over by a succession of leaders of the dynasty of David, and being preached to, criticized, and guided by a succession of prophets, and at the same time its people being led in their worship by generations of priests and Levites. The kingships of both Hezekiah and Josiah were deemed to be by the writers of the books of Kings particularly significant for their espousal of and leadership in the worship of the Lord God of Israel.

Yet there were other, and far greater, forces at work on the international scene. While an attempt by the Assyrian ruler Sennacherib to conquer Jerusalem in 701 BCE did not succeed, some years later in 586/7 BCE that city was captured and burnt, and many of its leaders were taken away into exile in Babylon and elsewhere. This time of exile lasted around fifty years, time enough for many of the Jewish people to become settled into their "new" surroundings, and for some to enter into marriages with Babylonian partners.

The Babylonian captivity of the people of Judah and Jerusalem came to an end with the conquest of Babylon by the Persian leader Cyrus, who wished to espouse a rather different policy concerning his subject peoples. He thus issued a decree allowing the Jewish exiles to return to Judah, permitting the rebuilding of the Jerusalem temple with costs, these costs according to Ezra 6:1–5 being met by the royal treasury of Babylon. Not surprisingly, there were conditions attached, in particular that Jewish people were to pay their taxes to the overlord, and further, were to pray for him. Thus took place the return of some of the Jewish exiles to Jerusalem and elsewhere in the old land of Judah, and in parts of the Old Testament we read of various outcomes as those returnees faced up to a new situation in what was for their people historically an old and much-loved setting. It would seem from the evidence we have that they were given a good deal of freedom and local autonomy. Much of these matters we read about in the books of Ezra and Nehemiah, and after these books the story is taken up both in the Apocrypha (that is, the Deuterocanonical books), and also in the Old Testament itself in the book of Daniel. The continuing story is that of the Greek kingdoms, which after the death of Alexander in 323 BCE became very harsh for the

Jewish people, they being put under great pressures to adopt thoroughgoing Hellenism along with the proscription of their traditional ways of Judaism.

This somewhat lengthy diversion into matters historical enables us to highlight some particular issues that do become evident in the pages of the Old Testament, not infrequently brought forth through the experiences of a series of succeeding historical circumstances and settings in which the Israelite and Judean peoples found themselves. These particular issues which are considered in what follows in this chapter are: The Gift of Land; The Matter of Change; Exile and the World View; Religious Faithfulness.

The Gift of Land

For some of us one of the most distressing issues of our own times is the fact that in the world of the twenty-first century, so many peoples are finding they must seek new lands where they can live their lives in freedom and in peace, and where they may find food and homes. Much the same concerns are to be found in various parts of the Old Testament, and certainly in these documents the whole theme of the gift of land is a matter perceived to be of great importance. Thus is the Lord God portrayed as in the beginning planting a garden in Eden, in the east, where he might put the human being he had made (Gen 2:8); all too soon having killed his brother, Cain is sent away to the land of Nod, east of Eden (Gen 4:16); Abraham in Gen 12 is sent to a new land that would be revealed to him. Later, so we are told in Gen 42, the brothers of Joseph, by that time experiencing conditions of famine in their own land, and having heard that there was in those days grain in Egypt, set off for that land to search for food—which indeed they did find. However later, their successors found unfavorable and unfriendly conditions in Egypt, and so embarked upon a great journey with many remarkable experiences as they travelled to the "promised land" of Canaan. It is a great, significant, and moving moment when the Israelite tribes cross the River Jordan, and under the leadership of Joshua, come into their promised land (Josh 1–3). Walter Brueggemann has written movingly about this recorded moment in the long history which the Old Testament tells of the divine gift of the land of Canaan to the people of Israel, saying,

> Nothing is more radical than this, that the sojourner becomes a possessor. The precarious sojourner has the heady new role of controller of what is promised and now given. The moment drastically redefines who Israel will be. Land entry requires of Israel that it cease to be what it has been in the wilderness and becomes what it had never been before.

And yet here in those affirmations there begin for us certain ethical problems, for we read in the book of Joshua of the apparently rapid defeat—through what is portrayed as great divine assistance—of the cities of Jericho (Josh 6) and Ai (Josh 8), and of other places, areas and establishments elsewhere in the land of Canaan. It does seem that Israel can only gain its own gift of the land through the wholesale destruction of the peoples who themselves were already occupying those lands. This is possible because, as the book of Deuteronomy expresses the matter, it is none other than the Lord God who clears away many nations before the Israelites—Hittites, Girgashites, Amorites, Canaanites and others—giving them over to the Israelites who can thus defeat them, indeed more than defeat them, in fact, so we are told, utterly destroying them (see Deut 7:1–2). Of course, it may be that we should accept that in the Old Testament's accounts of these events there is the element of exaggeration, but that hardly helps in the challenge of the ethics of all this. Does it not rather suggest that in order to exalt the power and authority of the Lord God in these accounts he is portrayed as deploying truly almighty powers and annihilating destructions upon the Canaanites so that his people Israel may come into residence—and possession—of the good and fruitful land of Canaan?

Surely, we have to accept that in matters of this nature we cannot take literally what the Old Testament has to say and apply it in simple ways to various situations in our world today. For truly in our contemporary world the whole issue of the gift and use of the land is of very great importance, and must inevitably be about how the lands of the world are to be equitably shared among all the different peoples, so many of whom are searching for a share of the space. For, with the passing of the ages and the increasing populations in the world, the whole matter of peoples finding peaceful and reasonably-sized shares of the gifts of land looks set to continue being problematic in the years to come. Further, the whole issue of national possessions of portions of the world's lands has changed from what it was in ancient times with the modern rise of nation states and the establishments of firm and fixed borders, so that populations can no longer move from area to area as, for example, the fortunes with crops and other foods changes. However in a most particular way the issue of land is as real as ever in those very lands that the Old Testament books of Deuteronomy and Joshua were written about, the so-called Holy Land. How tragically in those areas do the land disputes continue, indeed, looking set to continue for a long while yet.

Do we not have to acknowledge that some of the words of the Old Testament are not easily appropriated for adoption into our Christian spiritualities in the contemporary settings? Should we not say in such matters as these, that at times we do not find appropriate assistance and inspiration in the Old Testament scriptures, and that as regards these issues those who seek to lead lives of Christian spirituality must search elsewhere for guidance, both human and divine? We shall need to return to this issue in ch 7 below when we consider life with ethical concerns.

Change

The whole issue of change is undoubtedly problematical for religious people, maybe in particular for believers in the Judeo-Christian traditions. For are we not called in these religious traditions to find sure and strong roots and structures for our lives—both individually and corporately? Here in our scriptures we are assured are the great constants, the eternal verities, for our lives. Yet these are to be lived out it would appear so fleetingly in a constantly-changing world. There surely is the problem for us, the fact that things in the world are in constant upheaval, and we are thereby ever-being challenged, as to how we deal with such experiences. In fact, is the truth of the matter that religious people in the Judeo and Christian traditions do truly have to accept change in their lives? And if they do accept the possibility that in a worldly sense their lives are developing, are there then aspects of their religious beliefs, practices and actions that need to develop?

If we consider the New Testament documents we find that they all come from a reasonably modest time span, and that in the main they are concerned to speak of the significance of the coming into the world of Jesus Christ, in particular of the impact of his coming for individuals and communities. Perhaps the exception to this matter of the comparatively limited time-span of the New Testament writings is the book of Revelation, which it would be generally agreed comes from one of the times of persecution in the years of the early Church, and that did perhaps call for some adaptations and changes in the practices and observances of the still reasonably infant Christian Church. Apart from that, the New Testament documents are at pains to portray the great central and overwhelming significance of the Son of God who was born into the very midst of the world, who lived among us, who died our death and who by his resurrection from the dead opened the way for us to follow him into a future of hope.

How different is the Old Testament which covers such a large time span in the totality of its presentation. It seems reasonably clear that the materials of the Old Testament are by no means generally arranged in chronological order. Further, even those that are presented as representing a chronological scheme, may well be using materials that have come from different dates. Further it can at times be distinctly difficult to date materials used in such books as, for example, Leviticus. Moreover, when we are given detailed instructions about, say, ways of offering sacrifices, are we reading about what *did* happen in the past, or rather are we reading what the writer(s) believed *should* happen in the present and possibly also in the future?

However, in the matter of the people of Israel experiencing change, the reality of the enforced exile for a considerable number of them in Babylon and elsewhere clearly caused them to face up to the issues of change, of coming face to face with people of other ways of life, religious beliefs and maybe also world views. This demands a new section, as now follows.

Exile and World View

It is clear that the exile of Jewish people constituted an enormous change for the people of Judah and their leaders, bringing about the very considerable divide in the history of Israel, and in the thinking and proclamation of certain of the prophets and authors of biblical books. This was occasioned by the siege and fall of Jerusalem to the Babylonian army in 586/7 BCE and the taking into exile of certain of the Israelites and their leaders to Babylon and elsewhere. Further, the experience of exile, either as personally experienced, or else as having been informed about it—or indeed of the mere fact of it having taken place for some of their peoples—brought forth, perhaps inevitably, some differing views on the parts of those who afterwards wrote about these matters, both about telling what had happened in the past, and also for the purpose of conveying visions for the future existence of the people of Israel. For the fact is those who had been in exile and who thereby inevitably had to "rub shoulders" with peoples of different cultures, beliefs, and practices, had thus perhaps found themselves experiencing changes in their outlooks and views concerning the future. Further, would these people, even among themselves, have agreed about what should change, and where should development take place? Would we not expect there to be inevitable disagreements in such matters?

Thus, for example, a good deal, if not all, the material in Isa 56–66, it would be generally agreed, comes out of the exilic and post-exilic period and gives the appearance of being intended to be about the future life of the people of Israel when those people were back in their own land. These largely reassuring chapters surely present a real open, accommodating, even all-embracing spirit in regard to the future life in the old land of promise. Now—at least for this author (or authors)—how open and welcoming is the fellowship of the new place of worship in the restored Jerusalem in post-exilic days to be for all sorts and conditions of people: "my house shall be called a house of prayer for all peoples" (Isa 56:7), and perhaps even more, "And I will also take some of them as priests and as Levites, says the Lord." (Isa 66:21) Indeed here also we read,

> From new moon to new moon,
>   and from sabbath to sabbath,
> all flesh shall come to worship before me,
> says the LORD. (Isa 66:23)

What a far cry that particular contribution represents from the approach of the likes of Ezra and Nehemiah who stipulated that in returning to the land of Israel after the exile any marriages of Israelites to non-Jewish partners must be dissolved (Ezra 10:1–44; see also Neh 10:30; 13:23–30). Thus does the Old Testament in this instance present us with more than one point of view. The Old Testament cannot be said to be "united" around one viewpoint, a supposed official ruling, shall we say? The fact is, we are not being given in scripture for certain individual situations repeated offerings of the guidance and instructions that had been applied to an *earlier* situation, for now the situation may be different. Thus the prophetic word and the instruction, or the guidance, for the people of God has perhaps to be different from what had been given earlier. Rather, to speak more positively, what we do have here are some *new* insights, perhaps fresh adaptations of earlier instructions and practices, which in the opinions and understandings of some contemporary leaders, need accepting now in this new situation when the people of God have moved into new conditions, new settings in their lives.

It could be said that the experience of the exile led the people of Israel and their leaders into wholly new situations, situations that previously had been simply unexpected, fresh experiences that called forth some radically new thinking, in no small way including the embracing of a whole new world view, maybe a whole new appreciation of the Lord as God of the whole world. Surely, those famous four passages in Isa 40–55 about "the servant" who is called to the life of mission and servant-hood, suffering, and even death, must come out of the Israelite exilic experience and a divine call to a much wider vision of national witness and life in the future (Isa 42:1–4; 49:1–6; 50:4–9; 52:13—53:22). Surely the vision of the short book of Jonah about the call of an individual to go to a far country to proclaim a message about the care and concern of the God of Israel for all sorts and conditions and nationalities of people must also have come out of the Israelite exilic experience of having experienced life in a much wider and more cosmopolitan mix of peoples and nations.

The prophet of Isaiah chs 40–55 could see that with the accession to the throne in Babylon of Cyrus the Persian with his policy of allowing his captive peoples to return to their own lands certainly had presented the Jewish exiles with a remarkable new opportunity to return to their homeland with its capital city Jerusalem—although that city was in a somewhat ruinous state. With remarkable and compelling language the prophet of Isa 40–55 portrayed the moment as being like that of the exodus from Egypt, for he spoke thrillingly of a way being prepared for the people to travel through the desert places and so back to their old homeland. Thus a new situation presented a new—and surely previously unexpected—moment of opportunity to engage in a "new exodus." Indeed, once again a new and changed situation in the world presented the people of God with the challenge of doing some remarkable new things in their lives and in the ongoing corporate lives of their people. Hence, for example, this prophet proclaimed the Lord as saying nothing less than,

> Do not remember the former things,
>   or consider the things of old.
> I am about to do a new thing;
>   now it springs forth, do you not perceive it? (Isa 43:18–19)

Religious Faithfulness

Yet the above historical scenario would change again—and change dramatically. In fact, here in this further scenario is one of the major challenges for the people of God that are portrayed in the Old Testament. The new situation into which the people of God were propelled was the rule of the Greek Kingdoms, the military overlords who succeeded the Persians. We read about this period of Jewish life in the book of Daniel where the call to religious faithfulness is set forth in a number of different literary styles—all of them conveying vividly the religious challenge to the Jewish people of the day, and setting forth for the sympathetic reader the challenge of religious faithfulness in a situation in which there was serious opposition to Jewish practices by their rulers. The challenge of these times of Greek rule perhaps goes something like this: for how much of the time should the Jewish people be intermingling with those of other nations, cultures, experiences, and when might the moment have come that called for a stricter focus along with a standing firm upon their own traditions and beliefs? This is surely the great issue that is explored in the Old Testament book of Daniel. The background setting to at least parts of Daniel seems clearly to have been that of the Greek rule, in particular that of Antiochus IV, known as Epiphanes (175–164 BCE), who banned Jewish practices and desecrated the temple.

Daniel is here portrayed as determined to stand firm for his and his people's faith, and certainly not to worship Greek gods. Thus we have stories of the fiery furnace (Dan 3), and of Daniel being thrown into the den of lions (Dan 6), both of which searing experiences the religiously-faithful Jewish hero is portrayed as surviving—thus demonstrating that in his religious faithfulness is more help and strength than in the designs and devices of the Greek rulers. These—what are portrayed as being extreme sufferings and circumstances—were surely intended to be stories—encouraging stories—for those times when the life of the people of God and their faith in the Lord God were both alike under threat. Here were Jewish people being called upon to remain faithful in the beliefs and practices of their faith, and thereby to be reassured of hope for their own future and that of their faith.

The situation under the Greek rulers for the people of Israel was indeed extreme—in fact what is clearly the most extreme such situation portrayed in the books of the Old Testament. But it does serve to illustrate the challenge that in age after age there was the call to religious faithfulness for the people of God, whether those challenges came from the likes of a Queen Jezebel (see 1 Kgs 16:31; 18:4—21:25; 2 Kgs 9:7–37), or whether from the oppressive rule of an Antiochus Epiphanes, or whether from a general religious slackness in what were apparently more peaceful ages.

From Text to Spirituality

The subject matter of this chapter reminds us of the obvious fact that our Christian faith has to be lived out in the world, and that in this living out Christians are confronted with a series of challenges as to how that faith is to be practiced. The Old Testament certainly gives us a wide and varied conspectus of the settings and possible difficulties that Christians will find therein, right from the beginning as portrayed in the life to be lived-out in the Garden (Gen 1:1—4:26).

Thus there is a portrayed in the Old Testament the pressing need of the people of God, along with all other people, to have a reasonable and safe space of land for their lives, and further to be able to live in hope of a peaceful future. The Old Testament, further, gives eloquent witness to the necessity of appointing human leadership for a group of people, or even a nation, and that to be restrictive about powers vested in such persons may lead to their being unable satisfactorily to defend their peoples. On the other hand to give such leaders greater powers may inevitably invite or encourage them to assume too much to themselves, while at the same time perhaps to become less aware of the needs of those for whom they are responsible.

Further, there remain a series of challenges facing such a leader, namely that there are central aspects of the role of leadership which are to do with spiritual matters, and when, for example, in times of crisis what human action should be taken, and what should be sought from God through prayer, what guidance should be sought from a prophet or another religious leader. It can hardly be said that there is any resolution to these matters in the Old Testament nor that any clear answers are given, and yet in no small number of earthly and historical settings these matters are spoken about, frequently being discussed through the examples of actual happenings and crises.

Further, the Old Testament is not afraid to portray situations of change taking place in the world around the people of Israel. At times, no doubt, certain changes could perhaps be introduced into Israel's corporate life and practices, and that would be considered reasonable, even acceptable. Yet there may come some issue that in regard to various particular changes is unacceptable to some peoples. Thus all too easily can come about disagreements between, within peoples, and groups, which may or may not result in divisions.

Moreover, we should be aware of the fact that in some hypothetical issue possibly being experienced in the modern world there may be brought forth factors and issues quite different from those experienced in the world of ancient Israel. An example of this might be the emergence of the modern "nation state," with "closed" borders, along with the associated necessity of the possession of passports, or the equivalent, and close supervision of particular crossing places, lest individuals, peoples, communities not authorized to cross over find opportunity to do just that. Even so, we must surely still be aware of, indeed alert to, in a strongly sympathetic way, the issue of compassion and loving care on the part of the (comparatively) well-off for those who (comparatively) are suffering, and who even may be destitute. In this matter there must surely be compassion shown and exercised, even perhaps in those extreme situations when very large numbers of suffering peoples are involved. Further, while we may still have before us the story and the challenge of the Old Testament's Book of Ruth, and in particular the plight of Naomi and Ruth, we also have to accept that other aspects of the matter have undergone very great changes in the modern world.

The whole subject of "land" is a reminder to many of us in the contemporary world of the distressing fact that there are tragically so many peoples who continue to look for safe spaces in which they and their kindred may live in peace and hope, and that the mass movement of groups, and even nations, is now a much more fraught business than it was in earlier ages when those in need could move readily between areas and countries, and in some cases keep on moving as the local conditions changed.

There is also the religious issue that while human peoples must surely ever need a reasonable share of the earth's lands and provisions, yet the life of the people of faith is at the same time also a spiritual matter of our orientation to the divine, of the call to a religious faithfulness in age after age, and that there is a sense in which the Christian's dwelling place is both in the earthly dwelling and also, as the matter is expressed in Ps 90, in the Lord God. That is to say, there is the invitation to individuals and also to communities to live both physically on earth, each having a fair and reasonable share of the resources, but also a life of spirituality, one that is lived out in faith, hope and love in the Lord.

> The Lord said to him [Moses], "This is the land of which I swore to Abraham, to Isaac, and to Jacob, saying, 'I will give it to your descendants'; I have let you see it with your eyes, but you shall not cross over there." (Deut 34:4)

Further Psalm 90 speaks movingly and confidently of the eternity of the Lord's existence and presence with his people, in spite of all the chances and changes of the humans earthly lives:

> Lord, you have been our dwelling place
>   in all generations.
> Before the mountains were brought forth,
>   or ever you had formed the earth and the world,
>   from everlasting to everlasting you are God. (Ps 90:1–2)

Yet another witness of the community of faith about the life in a still-ever-changing world, and a world about which for individual people there must inevitably be so many unknowns concerning the future, is what was described long ago by one spiritual writer as "God, shrouded in the cloud of unknowing." As this unknown author of the work *The Cloud of Unknowing* expressed it:

> Yet I can show you something of these spiritual arts: at least I think so. Try them out, and see if you can do better. Do everything you can to act as if you did not know that they were so strongly pushing in between you and God. Try to look, as it were, over their shoulders, seeking something else—which is God, shrouded in the cloud of unknowing.

6

Life with Questions

I cry to you and you do not answer me;
I stand, and you merely look at me. (Job 30:20)

THE SHEER REALITY OF sufferings that come the way of apparently innocent peoples inevitably raises deep questions about the meaning and purpose of earthly life. If, further, those who are suffering are believers in a loving and caring God to whom they have entrusted their lives, the problem—at least theologically, spiritually—becomes the greater. For if God is believed to be all-loving, all-caring, all-powerful why do his people, his worshippers, his followers experience setbacks in their lives, some of them at times going through deep experiences of suffering? The above words come from the last of the many speeches of the suffering man Job in the Old Testament book named after him, and Job's continued complaint is that in spite of his many words to him, God does not seem to respond; rather the Lord appears merely to look at Job, neither to change his situation for the better, nor to give some explanation of why he is suffering so deeply. We shall return to the remarkable book of Job and all that it has to say through its various voices, but first we ought to consider what we may think of as some rather gentler Old Testament voices on this subject of human suffering, some perhaps rather less intense contributions to the subject.

So first, we go to the book called Ecclesiastes, which in the Hebrew is called Qoheleth, a name, or perhaps a title, or even a *nom de plume*, and which traditionally has been translated either as Teacher or Preacher. Qoheleth—for so we shall call him in this work—complains that there is a certain emptiness about life, a mysteriousness about it; things seem just to go, as we might express it, round and round in circles. There is a sense of emptiness, indeed vanity about life, thus in Eccl 1:2 we have (in the NRSV translation), "Vanity of vanities, says the Teacher, vanity of vanities! All is vanity." This is very much the theme of ch 1 of Ecclesiastes. Then in Eccl 3:16–22 the subject of justice comes up, for, says the writer, justice is not there in the world when you would expect it. What rather there *is* in the world is wickedness—that is in the place where one might have expected there to be realities like justice and righteousness. Thus,

> Moreover, I saw under the sun that in the place of justice, wickedness was there, and in the place of righteousness, wickedness was there as well. (Eccl 3:16)

Qoheleth's observations continue, in ch 6 coming to give expression to the observation: "There is an evil that I have seen under the sun, and it lies heavy upon humankind: those to whom God gives wealth, possessions and honor, so that they lack nothing of all that they desire, yet God does not enable them to enjoy these things, but a stranger enjoys them. This is vanity; it is a grievous ill." (Eccl 6:1–2) And something of a climax of this comes in 7:14 with its friendly advice, "In the day of prosperity be joyful, and in the day of adversity consider; God has made the one as well as the other, so that mortals may not find anything that will come after them." (Eccl 7:14) Life, Qoheleth seems to be saying, is like that; it has that unpredictable strain within it.

Yet it also has to be said that in spite of his questions and observations about life in the world with all its mysteries and much perplexity, Qoheleth continues to direct his reader's gaze towards God, and to a real sense of humility and reverence in their approach to him. Thus in 5:1 he counsels "Guard your steps when you go to the house of God", going-on to say that because God is in heaven and you are upon earth let your words be few (5:2), and somewhat climaxing his advice with the word "fear God" (Eccl 5:7).

Now the word fear in much of the Old Testament—and surely so in this passage—as we have already seen is not about being simply "scared" of God, but rather is about our being in *awe* of him, reverencing him. It is a fundamental word of the Old Testament about our approach to God, and it is also there in the New Testament. This is surely the sense of those followers of Jesus being "afraid" in what seems to be the last words St Mark wrote in his gospel account of Jesus (Mark 16:8), the reaction of the women who came to the tomb and found it empty, "and they said nothing to anyone, for they were *afraid*." (My italics).

Surely, Mark intends to convey to us that the women were filled with a sense of awe and reverence, for although they were in an earthly, geographical, physical setting yet they were receiving a great manifestation of the almighty and amazing work of God that had taken place. We are not surprised that they are recorded as having a deep, deep sense of awe!

And I suggest that there is this sense of awe in the short Old Testament book of Ecclesiastes expressed in the midst of all Qoheleth's somewhat agonized thoughts about the Lord and his ways on earth. Indeed Qoheleth ends his work on this note, with its

> "The end of the matter; all has been heard. Fear God, and keep
> his commandments; for that is the whole duty of everyone."
> (Eccl 12:13)

It should be noted that that final word places us firmly in our lives in the physical world, and at the same time suggests to us that our deepest understanding of things in the world will come from our orientation towards God, and what we today might call the spiritual aspects of our lives—in short our spirituality.

So we turn to the book of Psalms, in particular once again to that very large number of psalms in which an individual person laments the fact that for them so much in their lives seems to be going wrong, with so little going well. These have—very appropriately—been called Individual Lament psalms and in them we are hearing an individual lamenting their experience of very difficult life-circumstances. As we have also already considered, there are also in the Psalter what have been called Communal Lament Psalms, in which it seems a whole community is crying out to God and asking questions about "how long" they must endure their present difficult circumstances.

In many of these two groups of psalms the characteristic words, addressed to God, are "why?" and "how long?," and we should note that here we do have a very real outspokenness to God on the part of the suffering and confused individual or community. In no way does a psalmist say nothing, keep quiet! Rather, the suffering one, or indeed the community, hangs on to God—with at least *some* faith—speaking as if some answer is expected. If in fact any answer is given, we are not told about it, but what is clear is that in many an instance in these psalms there is a sense of peace about the problem on the part of the person concerned. Perhaps it is that having entrusted the deeply troublesome matter to God the person comes to a sense of peace. Though this does not happen in every case, it is there in many of them. Thus, for example in Ps 3 (an individual lament) we have the psalmist saying at the beginning,

O Lᴏʀᴅ, how many are my foes!
 Many are rising against me;
many are saying to me,
 "There is no help for you in God." (Ps 3:1–2)

Yet at the end the psalmist is saying,

Deliverance belongs to the Lᴏʀᴅ;
 may your blessing be on your people! (Ps 3:8)

Or we may consider Ps 43, noting in passing that in all probability Pss 42 and 43 made up the complete work. However, for our present purposes we consider only Ps 43, in particular noting the great change in mood on the part of the psalmist between its beginning and its end, though the latter is more in the sense of an anticipated good and satisfactory outcome of an earlier expressed sense of deep distress. Thus at first we have,

Vindicate me, O God, and defend my cause
 against an ungodly people;
from those who are deceitful and unjust
 deliver me! (Ps 43:1)

while at the end there is:

Why are you cast down, O my soul,
 and why are you disquieted within me?
Hope in God; for I shall again praise him,
 my help and my God. (Ps 43:5)

And we may finally with these lament psalms consider Ps 60, a psalm that is generally reckoned to be what has been called a Communal Lament. Here the whole community, perhaps even the whole nation, cries out to God that he will rescue them. Thus the psalm begins,

O God, you have rejected us, broken our defenses;
 you have been angry; now restore us!
You have caused the land to quake; you have torn it open;
 repair the cracks in it, for it is tottering.
You have made your people suffer hard things;
 you have given us wine to drink that made us reel. (Ps 60:1–3)

Yet in the last verse of this psalm is the note of confidence in God that he will surely rescue his people. It is as if this confident faith is being expressed by an individual who proclaims to the community,

With God we shall do valiantly;

it is he who will tread down our foes. (Ps 60:12)

What has actually happened for the psalmist, and how that happened, and equally what was the original problem, the crisis of life with which they were beset, we do not know. The fact is we are not told. Certainly in the individual laments we do not hear anything about the material situation for the psalmist, or for the community, or for others, physically changing, so what can have happened? Perhaps it was the fact that the psalmist having simply, and yet boldly, entrusted the troublesome matter to God was sufficient to bring peace and a deep sense of reassurance to that person. That is, what was maybe a physical problem, or series of problems, had been entrusted to God, and that through this spiritual activity things in life looked so much different, so much more manageable. As far as the problem spoken about in the communal lament in Ps 60 is concerned, perhaps the assurance was that with the divine help there would be deliverance effected through force of arms. Nevertheless, what we are witnessing in all of these lament psalms is the believed reality of the power and effectiveness of what we can only call a *spiritual* approach in the dealings either of an individual person or of a whole community with their problems in daily and worldly life. Here is a clearly expressed confidence on the part of both individuals and communities that there is indeed hope in the Lord for those who are beset with sufferings—namely that they entrust the troublesome matter to the Lord. That is, they are not called to put their trust in force of arms but rather in the care and gracious provision of God.

We shall stay for a while longer with the Old Testament Psalter, for we need to consider another group of psalms, those that have been labelled "Wisdom Psalms," this title having been given to a group of psalms that are dealing with those general themes of the Old Testament's so-called Wisdom Writings, namely questions about life and its purposes and meaning, and in particular why perhaps it is that there is suffering and distress in the world, and in the lives of certain individuals who appear to lead God-centered, God-fearing lives. However, it has to be said that there is a variety of scholarly opinions regarding the matter of just how many, and which, psalms should be regarded as belonging to this group. We shall consider here just three Wisdom Psalms, Pss 37, 49 and 73.

The subject being dealt with in Ps 37 is the apparent prosperity of the wicked, a matter that may bring about in the lives of at least some observers a sense of envy. Thus the psalm opens with the words,

Do not fret because of the wicked;
    do not be envious of wrongdoers ... (Ps 37:1)

And the counsel, or the instruction "Do not fret" is repeated in verses 7 and 8. However, the word translated "fret" perhaps needs something rather stronger in the English, more like, "fly into a passion," or even "be resentful." It has to be said that this psalm is somewhat limited in what it does have to say that may be of help to such "fretting" ones about the prosperity of the apparently wicked ones or the wrongdoers.

Nevertheless, these envious ones, fretting ones, are here assured a number of times in Ps 37 that they are to trust in the Lord (vv. 3, 5), more, that they are to delight in the Lord (v. 4), even that they are to commit their ways to him (v. 5). They are to remain quiet and patient before him (v. 7)—and of course they are not to fret (vv. 1, 7, 8). Rather they are to trust the Lord who is the all-powerful giver of all things (vv. 3, 9, 11)—and certainly not go in the ways of the wicked, those who surely live lives of great insecurity, lives that are without depth (vv. 9–10). Further, the psalm avers that the Lord will not allow the ways of the wicked to prevail (vv. 13–15), and they are not as strong as they may appear to be (vv. 16–17). What a contrast with the blessings of the devout (vv. 21–31) who can be sure that truly the Lord is their refuge:

> The salvation of the righteous is from the Lord;
> he is their refuge in the time of trouble.
> The Lord helps them and rescues them;
> he rescues them from the wicked, and saves them,
> because they take refuge in him. (Ps 37:39–40)

Such are the answers of the psalmist of Ps 37 to those righteous people who may ask questions of the Lord about some of the difficulties that they, the devout, find that they themselves—and maybe also others around them—are seeking.

Meanwhile, we go on to consider our second so-called Wisdom Psalm, namely Ps 49, in which the psalmist's concern is with those who appear to be his persecutors, being "those who trust in their wealth", those who "boast of the abundance of their riches" (Ps 49:6), those who find themselves in fortunate circumstances, namely, for whom "the wealth of their houses increases" (v. 16). How can the psalmist deal with this issue? First, and this is expressed in verses 5–12, is that the wealthy only have their wealth for a season, for the fact is that all, including the rich, die, "fool and dolt perish together and leave their wealth to others" (Ps 49:10). Further, the psalmist avers in verse 12, and will repeat these words in verse 20, "Mortals cannot abide in their pomp; they are like the animals that perish."

Then in verses 13–20 the psalmist says that while the wealthy have their possessions on earth, he, the psalmist, is blessed in a much greater way, namely,

> But God will ransom my soul from the power of Sheol,
>   for he will receive me. (Ps 49:15).

What is the psalmist saying here? Sheol in Old Testament thought is the place to which after death the humans go, for in much of these documents there is little about life after death. But it looks as if the psalmist of Ps 49 *does* have some thoughts about a life after death, but either cannot or does not choose to give any details. However, it is not without interest that in the case of the "passing" of Enoch, recorded in Gen 5:24, we have the same verb used as in Ps 49:15, a verb that can mean both "take" and "receive." This seems to be suggesting that there is maybe some thought here of a life after death—such as perhaps we read about in Ps 73:24 (see below); 2 Kgs 2:9–11; Isa 53:10–12—but about which nothing further can be said by these writers. But there is surely here some real expression of a future hope beyond death, and that those who may feel that they have somewhat missed out on the good things of earthly life may look forward with hope to future times and what under God they will bring.

So to our third of what have been called Wisdom Psalms, namely Ps 73, a psalm that is surely of real help to those faithful followers of God who have trouble with the apparent successes and large wealth acquisitions of some, while at the same time religiously faithful people who do not appear to make the same "progress" in life. But let the psalmist speak, first telling us what the established doctrine, the general religious understanding, is, and then going on to say just how he is feeling.

> Truly God is good to the upright,
>   to those who are pure in heart.
> But as for me, my feet had almost stumbled;
>   my steps had nearly slipped.
> For I was envious of the arrogant;
>   I saw the prosperity of the wicked. (Ps 73:1–3)

The psalmist then speaks about the lives and ways of the wealthy, about their pride, and about their violence at times (Ps 73:4–12), and how, in such apparent contrast, he—this humble psalmist—has tried to keep his heart clean, but who yet feels plagued and punished (vv. 13–14). Moreover, the psalmist says that he cannot by thinking about these matters make any progress, he is unable to understand what can be happening—he cannot, as we might say, get his head round the whole matter. "Until," he says, "until I went into the sanctuary of God; then I perceived their end." (v. 17) He came to see that the wicked were on something of what he calls a slippery slope, what will inevitably in the longer term lead to their downfall, an understanding that came to the psalmist in "the sanctuary of God", that is, we may imagine, in the Jerusalem temple, perhaps happening through his witnessing, or participating in, the worship there. Whatever it was, clearly something deeply religious, something spiritual, came to this person, so that he could see beyond this neighbor's worldly wealth and his own comparative earthly poverty (vv. 17–20). In fact, the psalmist came to see what a fortunate and privileged person he was in comparison with this man with all his worldly wealth, but otherwise sadly shallow existence. Thus the psalmist comes to utter one of the Old Testament's great confessions of faith and confidence—a confession that cannot but be quoted in full:

> When my soul was embittered,
>   when I was pricked in heart,
> I was stupid and ignorant;
>   I was like a brute beast towards you.
> Nevertheless I am continually with you;
>   you hold my right hand.
> You guide me with your counsel,
>   and afterwards you will receive me with honor.
> Whom have I in heaven but you?
>   And there is nothing on earth that I desire other than you.
> My flesh and my heart may fail,
>   but God is the strength of my heart and my portion forever.
> (Ps 73:21–26)

What did the psalmist mean by the words of v. 24, "and afterward you will receive [or, *take*] me with honor [or, *glory*]"? It sounds rather like that verse we noted above about Enoch not dying, but instead that God "took" or "received" (as we have seen, the Hebrew can mean either) him. Perhaps it may indeed be that the psalmist here is thinking about some sort of postmortem existence, but cannot give us any details. What however is surely clear is that there is a great sense of confidence on the psalmist's part: while he has little in life by earthly standards, the blessings he possesses of a spiritual nature are wondrously large and extensive—and possibly even eternal! Thus also, what frankly is amiss in his life when he does not have all that inevitably non-lasting worldly wealth possessed by that other person?

However, it is the book of Job that is the Old Testament's most extensive treatment of this whole subject of human suffering, along with the not-infrequent human feelings of either the absence of God from their life, or else some word or communication from him, to help them in their time of crisis. To this remarkable work we now turn.

The book of Job opens in the first two chapters with an account concerning how the good and religiously devout man Job (Job 1:1–5) came to suffer extra-ordinary tragedies and losses—the loss of his livelihood and the death of most of the members of his family (1:13–19). Then came the further problem for Job of a wretched skin disease (2:1–7), and yet at this time Job remained calm and collected in his relationship with God, still, we are told, remaining devout—in spite of his wife's advice that he should "curse God, and die" (2:9–10).

For we are also told in these opening chapters of the book that all this has taken place because, quite simply, the Lord God has allowed it to take place (1:6–12; 2:1–7).

We surely have to say that this apparently fantastical story of the cause of the sufferings of Job being due to divine authorization is singularly difficult for us both to read and also to believe. Must we not regard what we are reading in Job 1:6–12 and 2:1–7 as not intended to be understood either literally or historically, but that here we have a storyteller—an unknown storyteller for us—putting forth an example of the sorts of things that typically go wrong for people in the world, and to which religiously devout people are subject just as much as anyone else. This material, expressed in story-form, is intended to provide the necessary backdrop for the wide ranging debate and discussion that will follow through most of the rest of the book of Job, that is from 3:1–42:6. This latter is the heart of the book of Job, but the purpose of the opening story of how Job came to so many aspects of suffering is to set the scene for the forthcoming great debate about the sufferings of the apparent religiously devout people of earth. For further, as if to balance the "introductory story" there will be a "concluding story" in Job 42:7–17. But more of that later: first there is the large central part of the book, running from Job 2:11 right through to 42:6, and to this we now turn.

In Job 2:11–13 we read that three friends of Job—Eliphaz the Temanite, Bildad the Shuhite, and Zophar the Naamathite—having heard of the multitudinous calamities that had afflicted Job came to "console and comfort" him. This they did first, and this from a pastoral point of view they did quite excellently, by sitting with him a long time in silence—"and no one spoke a word to him, for they saw that his suffering was very great" (2:13). That silence is portrayed as being broken by Job speaking, speaking in a moving and heart-searching way of the sufferings that had recently come upon him and his family. So he cries out to God, cursing the day of his birth (3:1), saying,

Why did I not die at birth,
come forth from the womb and expire? (Job 3:11)

and ending with the words,

I am not at ease, nor am I quiet;
I have no rest; but trouble comes. (Job 3:26)

So the first of the friends of Job begins to speak, Eliphaz the Temanite, and it is a long speech that he makes (Job 4:1—5:27). Yet what he has to say can be expressed quite briefly, and is the statement that in God's world there is justice, and that it is innocent people who survive, but not those who are wicked. And this will be the point that each of the friends will make, through many words and lengthy speeches, to Job, the essentials being expressed thus,

Think now, who that was innocent ever perished?
Or where were the upright cut off?
As I have seen, those who plow iniquity
and sow trouble reap the same.
By the breath of God they perish,
and by the blast of his anger they are consumed. (Job 4:7–9)

This, it has to be said is a point of view found widely in the Old Testament, being particularly prevalent in the books of Kings; in the case of many of the kingships in both of the states of Israel and Judah their lack of prosperity, well-being or success so frequently, if not usually, being explained by whether they were, or whether they were not, faithful to the ways of the Lord. See, for example, the explanation in 2 Kgs 21:12–15 for the fall of Jerusalem to the Babylonians being explained as due to lack of human faithfulness to the Lord God. This point of view is also to be found, for example, in the book of Lamentations (see for example Lam 1:5), in the so-called Wisdom literature, and also in the books of the prophets. Yet it surely does have to be said that this is not always true, for we observe situations in life where some people commit great evils in life, while living what look like successful lives, and that equally there are apparently innocent, good-living people who suffer enormous difficulties, or inexplicable illnesses, some of them great deprivations. Many people in their lives just do not seem to deserve either their share of sufferings or alternatively their outstandingly good fortunes. This cannot be reckoned to be an adequate explanation for the sufferings of righteous people.

Job responds to Eliphaz's (long) speech in Job 6:1—7:21, but it hardly either answers Eliphaz's points, or accepts the force of his argument and viewpoint. Rather, Job continues to talk of his troubles and his associated lack of hope:

> My days are swifter than a weaver's shuttle,
>   and come to their end without hope. (Job 7:6)

Then follows Bildad the Shuhite's first speech in Job 8:1–22. This, it has to be said, very much repeats the view of Eliphaz and brings very little that is new, and in fact the same very much applies also to the third of the friends in his speeches, Zophar the Naamathite. This is indeed the point of view of Job's so-called friends. Yet at the same time Job's speeches in his responses to the "friends'" contributions become more complaining, disputatious and argumentative. He feels that he is very much being pursued by God without mercy (7:11–16), and that if he really has sinned so greatly cannot God forgive him, while God has time—that is, before Job dies? (7:16) Later, Job comes to see that he as a mere mortal cannot find adequate words with which to address the Lord (9:14–15), and he comes to wish that there would be someone, some person, who could in these matters be the "umpire" between himself and the Lord (9:33). Job does indeed say later, 16:19 that he has a "witness" in heaven, and we do wonder who might be intended by this word: is it the "umpire" of 9:33, or is it perhaps even God—the Lord?

Yet when we get to chapter 19—a chapter making up all of one of Job's speeches—there is expressed what looks like a growing confidence in finding help in God, in fact finding God to be on his (Job's) side. This is not an easy passage to translate, not least because we do not know what is intended by some of the words in it—such as, for example "Redeemer" of v. 25—but the following is the translation found in the New Revised Standard Version.

> O that my words were written down!
>   O that they were inscribed in a book!
> O that with an iron pen and with lead
>   they were engraved on a rock forever!
> For I know that my Redeemer lives,
>   and that at the last he will stand upon the earth;
> and after my skin has been thus destroyed,
>   then in my flesh I shall see God,
> whom I shall see on my side,
>   and my eyes shall behold, and not another.
> My heart faints within me! (Job 19:23–27)

To cut a long story short—and summarizing a great deal of Old Testament scholarship—it would seem that what is intended here by "Redeemer" (Job 19:25) is nothing less than God himself; and that when Job says he will know the Redeemer while he (Job) "stands upon the earth" means while Job is still alive in his earthly life. Further, he will see him on his side—that is Job will see God here *on earth*. Even so, a little later Job says he would so much wish to come before God, presenting his case to him.

> Oh, that I knew where I might find him,
>> that I might come even to his dwelling!
> I would lay my case before him,
>> and fill my mouth with arguments. (Job 23:3–4)

Even so, Job is aware that to see God will be a truly awesome experience:

> These are indeed but the outskirts of his ways;
>> and how small a whisper do we hear of him!
> But the thunder of his power who can understand? (Job 26:14)

Yet now, something new happens in the book of Job. With chapter 28 we have a poem on the subject of where will wisdom be found; where is the place of understanding? There are those who have the skills to dig mines deep into the earth. Have they come to wisdom, that is understanding about the deep things of life, the things about God, what earthly existence is all about? (Job 28:1–11) No, the real wisdom is not here in the depths, in the mines, or in the seas (28:12–14), nor cannot it be bought (vv. 15–19), it cannot be found in the skies (v. 21), in fact not even has death found it (v. 22). Rather, only God knows about this (vv. 23–27), and further it is only through human awe of God, human reverence of God—that true sense of the "fear" of the Lord—that we shall come to any real understanding of God, the universe—and everything else; all this only through our holding God in a deep sense of awe, and our departing from all that is not of God, that is sin and evil. Thus,

> And he said to humankind,
>> "Truly, the fear of the Lord, that is wisdom;
>> and to depart from evil is understanding." (Job 28:28)

Now Job speaks again, and he speaks at length, from Job 29:1 to 31:40. In fact this will be the last time he speaks at length, we being told at the end of Job 31:40, "The words of Job are ended." This is not strictly accurate for Job will speak after each of the speeches of the Lord, but that will be in exceedingly few words and in a spirit of deep humility and penitence (Job 40:3–5; 42:2–6). Meanwhile Job reiterates his general feelings, among much else saying,

> O that I had one to hear me!

> (Here is my signature! Let the Almighty answer me!)
> O that I had the indictment
> written by my adversary! (Job 31:35)

So now we hear a new voice, this being the voice of Elihu son of Barachel the Buzite, one who acknowledged that because he was young in years he was timid and afraid, for the others (presumably he means the other speakers) were aged (Job 32:6). But in fact Elihu does have something new to say in the great debate about the experience of suffering on the part of apparently good and devout people, and his utterances run from Job 32:1—37:24. Elihu's central point of view is that suffering may in fact be for the sufferer a divine discipline, perhaps a divine education. This "explanation" for suffering has been very briefly aired earlier in the book of Job by Eliphaz, who in his first speech (Job 4:1—5:27) says,

> How happy is the one whom God reproves;
> therefore do not despise the discipline of the Almighty.
> For he wounds, but he binds up;
> he strikes, but his hands heal. (Job 5:17–18)

This is what comes out, perhaps somewhat repetitively, in Elihu's speeches, particularly in Job 33:13–18; 34:31–37; 36:7–13, 15–16, and we may feel that it has a certain value in being set forth, but maybe not too much. This is what in the hands of the poet John Keats became the plea not to call the world a "vale of tears," but rather "The vale of Soul-making," but it is there in Elihu's contribution to Job's problem,

> He delivers the afflicted by their affliction,
> and opens their ear by adversity.
> He also allured you out of distress
> into a broad place where there was no constraint,
> and what was set on your table was full of fatness. (Job 36:15–16)

There are other things that are set forth in the words of Elihu, such as for example among his opening words are these:

> But truly it is the spirit in a mortal,
> the breath of the Almighty, that makes for understanding. (Job 32:8)

This appears to be saying that there is something quite particular, and deeply significant, about this spiritual gift of the Lord to the human beings. Later Elihu will say that the spirit of God had made him (Elihu) and that the breath (or "spirit") of the Almighty had given him life (Job 33:4), and saying further,

> If he should take back his spirit to himself,
>   and gather to himself his breath,
> all flesh would perish together,
>   and all mortals return to dust. (Job 34:14–15)

This "spirit," this "breath" is portrayed as being vital to human life, that which makes them living beings (as in Gen 2:7), and as something more than the physical human breathing that it seems is being spoken of in Isa 42:5 and Ps 104:29. This is what we mean by the assertion that the humans are capable of being *spiritual* beings, those who are gifted with a spiritual relationship with the Lord, those who in our language of today can have a "spirituality."

It also needs to be said that perhaps significant is the placing of the contributions of Elihu just before that moment when Job needs to be prepared to meet with God. Thus Elihu says near the end of all his words, "Hear this, O Job; stop and consider the wondrous works of God" (Job 37:14), a little later completing his speeches with the words,

> The Almighty—we cannot find him;
>   he is great in power and justice,
>   and abundant righteousness he will not violate.
> Therefore mortals fear him;
>   he does not regard any who are wise in their own conceit. (Job 37:23–24)

And thus—and at last!—the Lord speaks to his suffering, and we imagine somewhat bewildered, servant Job. We last heard of Job saying those words quoted above, "O that I had one to hear me!" (Job 31:35), and now finally the Lord does speak to the suffering man, but alas! God does not speak about any of the troublesome and mysterious matters that have come into Job's life. Rather, this speech of the Lord (38:1—40:2) is about what God has done in the creation of the world, and in his maintenance of its governance. One cannot help feeling that the underlying theme of this speech is that God really does know what he is doing in his works of creation and maintenance of the creation—matters which frankly Job, and all the others of the humans, have neither the competence nor the power to do themselves.

It should also be noted that the Lord is portrayed as speaking here "out of the whirlwind" (Job 38:1), and it would seem that we are intended to understand that this is another of the Old Testament's mighty appearances of God—theophanies—like those recorded in Ezek 1:4 and Zech 9:14. Job is not given answers to his questions about life on earth, but rather is being confronted with the sheer greatness, authority and power of God, being confronted with something deep about the mystery of the Lord's otherness from all things earthly.

Thus is Job deeply humbled—and as good as lost for words—all he can say being,

> Then Job answered the LORD:
> "See, I am of small account; what shall I answer you?
> I lay my hand on my mouth.
> I have spoken once, and I will not answer;
> twice, but will proceed no further." (Job 40:3–5)

Here is a frail, earthly, ignorant human being before the holy God of all times and all worlds, and rightly and understandably Job is silenced. We are reminded of the call of the prophet Habakkuk to his people before the Lord appears in response to their entreaties. So Habakkuk counsels,

> But the LORD is in his holy temple;
> let all the earth keep silence before him! (Hab 2:20)

Then the Lord speaks *again* to Job (Job 40:6—41:34), and here we read about the great monsters, Behemoth (40:15–24) and Leviathan (41:1–34), great creatures, the first of the land, the second of the seas, and the clear suggestion here is that these have not only been created by God, but also are mysteriously and remarkably under the control of, subject to the authority of the Lord. Both land and sea, and all that is on or in them have been created by the Lord, and both, indeed *all things*, are under the divine rule.

Thus Job makes his confession of faith in God, about whom he has come to see that it is he, the Lord, who can do all things, and that none of his purposes can be thwarted (Job 42:2). Further, Job comes to the awareness that he has been speaking about things of which he in fact never actually understood—"things too wonderful for me, which I did not know" (Job 42:3). Which leads Job to say to the Lord,

> I had heard of you by the hearing of the ear,
> but now my eye sees you;
> therefore I despise myself,
> and repent in dust and ashes. (Job 42:5–6)

The book of Job comes to its conclusion with two more small pieces. The first of these is the note about the Lord's anger against Job's so-called friends, Eliphaz, Bildad and Zophar for having spoken incorrectly about the things of God. Thus is Job to seek forgiveness for them through sacrifice and prayer, which we are told the Lord accepted (Job 42:7–9). Secondly, we are told that the Lord restored the fortunes of Job after all these happenings and all the very many words. This may seem to many of us to be a somewhat problematical ending to the book—a "happy ending," when in fact the whole book has led us back not just to where the man Job and his family were at the beginning of the work, but in fact to a much deeper probing into some of the great issues of life. The whole purpose of the work is intended to survey some of the most difficult aspects and mysteries of earthly life, and thereby has led us to new depths in the spiritual life. We can understand that the book began with the scene-setting of an earthly tale of tragedy, and perhaps at the conclusion of the work that did need a satisfactory earthly ending. Yet for many of us the great contribution of the book to our lives lies in the *spiritual* realm, in the fact that this remarkable book tells of a man who came to a very deep enrichment of his life, and that through our reading of this old, old tale we are invited to be led through suffering to the deep enrichment of our fellowship with God and to the probing of new depths in our spirituality. Thus surely, the heart of the book is not dependent upon having an earthly "happy ending" but rather upon coming to new realms in the spiritual life that will enable a suffering people to come to a sense of peace and hope, and above all to a new relationship with their Lord.

So to another of the Old Testament's contributions to the whole issue of believers in the Lord God experiencing sufferings, namely the second part of the book of Isaiah, that is chapters 40–55, which it is very widely agreed come from the closing years of the Babylonian exile of the Jewish people. The background to these chapters would seem to be in Babylon in the reign of the ruler Cyrus (see Isa 44:28; 45:1) and that a moment has come when there could be new life back in Israel by what is portrayed in the language of a new exodus (Isa 40:3–11; 43:14–19). However, these thrilling chapters—for they are indeed thrilling with their promise of new hope and new life—are punctuated by four passages which speak of witness and service, and also of suffering. These are Isa 42:1–4; 49:1–6; 50:4–9; and 52:13—53:12, and these have been studied over the years in quite enormous detail. The point of view taken in this present work is that these four passages are intended by this prophet of the exile to speak about the life of servanthood and suffering that the people of Israel in future days may have to endure. It is the third and the fourth of these "servant passages" that speak of the sufferings of the un-named servant, and I am particularly concerned here with the fourth of them, namely Isa 52:13—53:12. I have argued elsewhere that that this passage is intended to present the prophet's vision that the future following of the Lord would involve them in suffering. In no way would their path in life back in the old Israelite homeland be a triumphant ruling over other peoples as it had been at certain times in the past (in particular, historically during the kingships of David and Solomon), but would inevitably be a way of servanthood and suffering. This is spoken about in Isa 53:1–3, 7–9, and it would appear that even death is being envisaged in vv. 7–9. Yet at the same time, Isa 53:10–11 seems to be envisaging a life *after* death, in particular through the words about the servant, that "out of his anguish he shall see light" (v. 11). Here is one of those somewhat few places in the Old Testament where a belief in a future life is given expression, and it surely represents a real source of hope to those who suffer in their lives of faithfulness and discipleship in the Lord's name. The portrayal of future life would seem to be expressed in somewhat halting language, for perhaps quite simply the writer was greatly challenged in seeking to give expression to these new and radical thoughts, in fact new understandings of what the life of faithfulness to God might both involve and also promise.

There are indeed a few other places in the Old Testament where the possibility of a life after death is given expression, one of these being in the book of Daniel where we read,

> Many of those who sleep in the dust of the earth shall awake, some to everlasting life, and some to shame and everlasting contempt. Those who are wise shall shine like the brightness of the sky, and those who lead many to righteousness, like the stars forever and ever. (Dan 12:2–3)

This speaks with confidence that those who have lived faithfully on earth do have a relationship with the Lord that transcends earthly death and that they will inherit a new life—of which no details are given—in a new environment. And briefly to complete this survey of "late" materials in the Old Testament we may notice the words of such hopeful assurance in Isa 26:19 about "your dead shall live, their corpses shall rise . . . and the earth will give birth to those long dead." Yet, it must once again be stressed that these verses are very generally believed to be what we would consider late additions to the Old Testament texts that have been passed down to us. But they do thus afford some real new hope for those who find that their faithful discipleship and following of the Lord may bring to them extremes of suffering, even including death, and this is a matter to which we shall return in ch 8 below.

From Texts to Spirituality

Suffering has been a reality all through the ages for all sorts and conditions of people, and it presents a particular problem for religious people who may feel that they are held in the safe keeping of a deity. Certainly, the theme of suffering and the problems thereof for devout followers of the Lord is firmly there in various parts of the Old Testament, but these documents are hard put to come up with any adequate explanations for their existence. What however can be said is that in the Old Testament there are two main matters that are maintained, the first being that the Lord is aware of his people's sufferings, and in the witness of those experiences when individuals are portrayed as crying out to the Lord about their difficulties in life they do, mysteriously, come to a sense of peace, even hope. This we have seen in particular ways in what we read in Ps 73, and also in the book of Job, in the latter in particular when the Lord makes himself known to the suffering and tortured man. No "solution" to the problem is given, and yet the human individuals do come to a sense of peace and acceptance. This is to say that any sense of hope in the midst of suffering is portrayed in the Old Testament as lying in what we might call the spiritual realm. For it is not that in any way the lots and fortunes of the people concerned have changed, and nor have they come to any new understandings as to why such things should have been happening in their lives. And yet the Old Testament can speak of them coming to a sense of spiritual peace, which is perhaps to say that any "answers" about our human and earthly sufferings have to come to us in the realm of our spirituality, in what is for each of us our spiritual lives.

Robert Gordis said finely in his helpful study of the book of Job,

> The poet's ultimate message is clear: Not only *Ignoramus*, "we do not know," but *Ignorabimus*, "we may never know." But the poet goes further. He calls upon us *Gaudeamus*, "let us rejoice," in the beauty of the world, though its pattern is only partially revealed to us. It is enough to know that the dark mystery encloses and in part discloses a bright and shining miracle.

It has been said that the Old Testament testifies to two contrasting aspects of spirituality, namely hope and confidence on the one hand, crisis and conflict on the other. This is not to be denied, but what surely further needs to be said is that the Old Testament also speaks about those two aspects of spirituality coming together, as we have seen in the texts we have considered in this chapter. Yet perhaps this can be hardly better expressed than it was in the above quotation from the work of Robert Gordis, "It is enough to know that the dark mystery encloses and in part discloses a bright and shining miracle."

Perhaps there is also a word for us once again in those *Revelations of Divine Love* of Julian of Norwich, where we are told,

"And you shall see yourself that all manner of things shall be well." I understand this in two ways: first, I am well pleased that I do not know it; second, I am glad and happy because I shall know it. It is God's wish that we should know in general terms that all shall be well; but it is not God's wish that we should understand it now, except as much as is suitable for us at the present time, and that is the teaching of Holy Church.

7

Life with Ethical Concerns

> You shall not take vengeance or bear a grudge against any of
> your people, but you shall love your neighbor as yourself: I am
> the LORD. (Lev 19:18)

BY "ETHICS" WE MEAN the subject, with all its many questions, of what is
right, what is good in the living of our lives in our communities and in the
world; or to express it briefly, how we should behave. In particular, speaking
in a religious context, ethics is about our attempts to live our earthly lives
in the closest possible conformity to the will of God. The above verse from
the Old Testament book of Leviticus calls upon us, in what is set forth as
a command of none other than the Lord God to his people, to love our
neighbor as we love ourselves. In the Old Testament documents ethical and
religious concerns are very much bound up together, what are matters of
right moral conduct are not distinguished from what are matters of right
religious conduct; in the Hebrew Bible ethics and conduct in life are bound
up with faith and belief.

Yet it has to be said that at times the Old Testament would seem to be
giving us some rather strange, sometimes difficult, even at times singularly
perplexing, guidance about loving our neighbors as ourselves. If we read
on in the book of Leviticus from the above quotation in Lev 19:18, we shall
soon come across talk of the death penalty for certain abuses of sexual relationships, such as adultery (Lev 20:10), homosexuality (Lev 20:13), incest
(Lev 20:11), bestiality (Lev 20:15–16). Other misdemeanors, the people
were warned, could land them with the fate of being stoned, such as idolatry

(Deut 13:6–11), or blasphemy (Lev 24:14), even for the persistent rebellion of a son against his parents (Deut 21:18–21).

In other parts of the Old Testament there would seem to be disproportionate statements such as that of the prophet Amos with his assertion "Does disaster befall a city, unless the LORD has done it?" (Amos 3:6). Even the psalms can at times appear to fall below their most tender, thoughtful, and fine words with certain expostulations against such crimes as the Edomite occupation of parts of Jerusalem while the Israelites were held as exiles in Babylon—see Ps 137:7–9. Nor do Christians find it easy to read in the Old Testament some matters concerning what have been called "holy wars" where there might be the command to annihilate the residents of an Israelite city previously occupied by non-Israelite people, such as we find, for example, in the case of the taking and occupation of Jericho in Josh 6:1–27. Indeed the whole section of the book of Joshua chs 6–11 gives us a somewhat gruesome, and certainly troubling, picture of the people of Israel being involved in a "holy war" against the indigenous population of the land, complete with divine instructions to kill all men, women and children, as also we read did take place following on from the successful Israelite conquest of Jericho (see Josh 6:21). While the Old Testament has a timely reminder for us about the care of immigrants and refugees (see for example Lev 19:9–10; 23:22; Deut 24:19b–22), we can hardly say the same about its talk of the living God in the age after the exodus from Egypt and the apparent long desert march "who without fail will drive out from before you the Canaanites, Hittites, Hivites, Perizzites, Girgashites, Amorites, and Jebusites" as the Israelites under the leadership of Joshua take possession of the land of Canaan (Josh 3:10–11). Further, some of the portrayed great leaders of Israel, certain of them presented as the Old Testament's outstanding models of faith, are at times hardly presented as being exemplars of good ethical conduct—there are those who commit adultery (David; see 2 Sam 11); who murder (Moses, Exod 2:11–15); who deceive (Jacob, Gen 27:1–29). Then too we read of the killing of the Egyptian firstborn children (Exod 12:29), and also the later destruction of the Egyptian army (Exod 14).

Bearing in mind these sorts of considerations, and the somewhat inevitable limitations that they must place upon our use of the Old Testament in the making of ethical decisions about the living out of the spiritual life in the contemporary world, is there in fact any worthwhile purpose in our looking for help in the Old Testament in this regard? I suggest that there are at least four particular ways in which we may consult these documents as we seek to make our ethical decisions in the world of today. These are offered as four different approaches to the varied and at times scattered Old Testament materials concerned with what we call ethical matters. At times there will appear to be certain repetitions in what is being said, due to some varied ways of coming at the same pieces of biblical material. The first of these concerns the case of certain people who are in particular situations of need; the second is about matters to do with the search for and administration of justice; the third is about the human attempt to imitate God in his care of his people; the fourth is about our seeking guidance from the Old Testament for our ethical living today. So, to the first of these ethical emphases we come across in the Old Testament, the care of those who have in their lives some particular needs.

Those in Need

The Old Testament, particularly in some of its books, makes clear a deep concern for the less-fortunate in the Israelite society, especially those who are poor, who are dispossessed, those who lack justice in their lives. For example, in the first chapter of the book of the prophet Isaiah, a chapter that is widely regarded as being in the nature of an introduction to the whole work of sixty-six chapters, there are a number of verses specifically concerned with doing good for other people, in particular for those who are suffering difficulties and setbacks in their lives. Thus we read,

> Wash yourselves; make yourselves clean;
>   remove the evil of your doings
>   from before my eyes;
> cease to do evil,
>   learn to do good;
> seek justice,
>   rescue the oppressed,
> defend the orphan,
>   plead for the widow. (Isa 1:16–17)

The end of the preceding verse (Isa 1:15) had carried the charge that the peoples' hands were covered with blood, that those hands had been used in the carrying out of unholy, even immoral acts. Here in v. 16 the command is that such persons are to wash their hands before they come to the Lord in worship—that is they are to take steps to undergo an inner, spiritual moral cleansing. We are reminded of Ps 15, a psalm that has been called an "Entrance Liturgy," that is a liturgy intended to be performed before a person goes before the Lord in worship. Now what is surely interesting about this liturgy, as we have earlier observed, is that it is entirely about practical matters, in particular being about the sort of lives that those coming to worship have been living in the world. The concern in Ps 15 seems to be entirely about the worldly lifestyle of the worshipper; for nothing is said in this psalm about the appropriateness of this or that prayer, or of this or that particular sacrifice the worshipper might be wishing to offer.

Thus here also in Isa 1:16–17 the emphasis is upon correct living in the world, upon learning to do good, about seeking for justice in the national community—that is working for fair and reasonable shares in earthly life for all people, in particular perhaps for those who are neither influential nor powerful. Those who would worship the Lord must first do what they can to rescue the oppressed, to defend the orphan, and to plead for the widow—and that perhaps means for later generations the pleading for similarly suffering people in each age and culture.

The same emphasis is to be seen in the book of the prophet Amos, in particular in that striking passage about the Lord not desiring from his people either their keeping of festivals or engaging in other solemn assemblies, even making various sacrificial offerings (Amos 5:21–22), or the singing of songs, or the playing of musical instruments (v. 23); rather what the Lord requires is justice and righteousness from his people. See, for example, Amos 5:24 and Mic 6:8.

Further, the striving of a faithful individual to have this purity of life which leads to a real sense of care for other members of the community, which can indeed make real demands upon the people of God, is to be observed in the Old Testament in such texts as, for example, Ps 73:13; Job 15:14 and Prov 20:9. Another series of texts concerns those in the community who are in debt and who do not have the financial means to pay off their debts, and this is where the concept of the seventh year—that is the Sabbatical year—being a time when there is to be what the New Revised Standard Version translates as "remission of debts" (Deut 15:1). We have a certain difficulty in understanding what it is precisely that the Old Testament is saying here, because the Hebrew word translated "remission" can mean either "suspension" (perhaps for a year?) or "termination" of debts. Thus while the spirit of the law may be all too clear to us, at the same time we have to confess ignorance of more precise details. In particular, are we intended to be thinking of a suspension of a debt, or it is a wiping out of it? We also read about the Sabbatical year in Exod 23:11; 31:12–17 and in Lev 25:1–17, 20–22.

Then in the book of Leviticus we read about a Jubilee year, namely the year after seven Sabbatical years, which is to say the fiftieth year. This is detailed only in Lev 25, especially in verses 8–55. During this particular year not only are the Israelites commanded to let the land lie fallow, but also are charged with using it as the opportunity when inequalities in the social order could be righted, when there could be remission of debts, the liberation of slaves, and the return of family property to its original ownership. Whether all, or much, of this actually took place is questionable, for it has to be said that we do not in any of the Old Testament books read about it explicitly being put into effect. Nevertheless, we should perhaps be very grateful for, and mindful of the fact that it is there in the Old Testament as an aspect of a great and fine vision of a just and caring society, one of high morality, a life certainly not devoid of high ethical considerations.

We should also take notice when in at least one place the Old Testament gives a vision of the king taking care of those of his people who are needy, and perhaps poor. This is Psalm 72, one of the so-called Royal Psalms, namely psalms that are about the Israelite king's high calling and very great responsibilities. Psalm 72 verses 2 and 4 speak hopefully that the king will judge the poor with justice, defend their cause, that he will give deliverance to the needy and "crush the oppressor," such "oppressors" presumably being those who would themselves have the power to crush the weak, the needy, the poor (Ps 72:4). The theme is renewed in verses towards the end of the psalm, which read as follows,

> For he [the king] delivers the needy when they call,
> the poor and those who have no helper.
> He has pity on the weak and the needy,
> and saves the lives of the needy.
> From oppression and violence he redeems their life;
> and precious is their blood in his sight. (Ps 72:12–14)

These matters are part of the Old Testament's vision of the responsibilities of the Israelite king, to have this sort of care for the poor of his people, to ensure that proper and appropriate provision is made for them—especially by those who have the powers and the wealth to do so! So also, the poor are spoken of in the book of Isaiah's vision of a coming ideal king (Isa 11:4), and moreover in various of the biblical psalms (see, for example, Pss 41:1; 82:3–4), and further in no small way in the book of Proverbs where the contrasting situations of the wealthy and the poor are set forth (see in particular Prov 14:31; 17:5; 22:2). Nor to be forgotten is that scene portrayed in the book of Ruth, of Ruth working in the field of a certain Boaz, in the time when she and Naomi had come to Judah to find food when that was not available in Moab. (Ruth 2:1–7) Naomi had originally come from Judah, but Ruth was from Moab, and so was an "alien." Ruth must harvest some of that corn which the people of Israel were commanded was to be left at the edges of the fields for just such people in need, as we read,

> When you reap the harvest of your land, you shall not reap to
> the very edges of your field, or gather the gleanings of your har-
> vest. You shall not strip your vineyard bare, or gather the fallen
> grapes of your vineyard; you shall leave them for the poor and
> the alien: I am the LORD your God. (Lev 19:9–10; see also Lev
> 23:22 and Deut 24:19b-22)

Are not these matters adequately set forth in the Old Testament so making the point clear to its readers that in various parts of its writings it does truly have a deep concern for the poor of the land, even for the alien, and that it is not without a moral code and standards for those in its midst who are needy? Thus we may go on to make the following observations which follow naturally from the above.

The Administration of Justice

In the preceding section we have come across the talk of a people who find themselves in situations and circumstances of need, for whom the Old Testament can speak of the provision of necessities that may relieve them of their present difficulties to at least some extent. No doubt, there will inevitably be at certain times those who find themselves in continuing situations of need, and in this regard we have come across the word "justice." Yet something more needs to be said about this word, and the whole concept it is intended to indicate, namely, the great importance of the pursuit of the reality of *justice*—this to be ideally in the lives of *all* the people of Israel.

As far as the portrayed early periods of Israel's history are concerned, we read about family and tribal leaders being spoken of as acting like judges (see, for example, Gen 38:24), and later in the wilderness traditions we hear of Moses himself being the judge of his people, until others were appointed to help him, while Moses' own particular role was with the larger cases as they came along (Exod 18:22). Yet clearly here was a matter that required near constant supervision, for we are not without evidence in the Old Testament to suggest that from various periods things in this regard were not working out as was intended. For example, in the first chapter of the book of Isaiah we have what amounts to a rebuke of the Lord God for those in Jerusalem who are not administering justice as they should be doing. The prophet looks back and speaks of how in earlier times there was a faithful city, but which alas has now become more akin to a "harlot" or a "gang of murderers" (Isa 1:21), indeed further, how the princes are rebels and friends of thieves, those who in particular are failing to defend the cause of the orphans and the widows (v. 23). Yet all these people have been shown how they should behave and live out their lives in the community of the people of Israel, that is in the same way as the Lord God has himself acted towards his people in nothing less than justice and righteousness:

> The LORD of hosts is exalted by justice,
> and the Holy God shows himself holy by righteousness. (Isa 5:16)

These two words, "justice" and "righteousness" at times appear together in the Old Testament, and they do indeed have closely similar meanings, perhaps being intended to give emphasis to the matter of there being correct relationships between the various members and groupings of the Israelite community. It is intended that there should be right and good relationships between the people themselves, and also between the leaders and their peoples. There are parts of the Old Testament documents that set this forth as an important matter, that there should ever be a real search for a sense of equality and freedom for all people in the life of the Judean society, and in particular for those who are not at present experiencing these things in their lives. Thus, for example, the book of Deuteronomy speaks about the justice of God (see Deut 32:4), saying also that this justice is what God calls for from his people in their corporate lives, "Justice, and only justice, you shall pursue, so that you may live and occupy the land that the LORD your God is giving you." (Deut 16:20)

Then there is righteousness, which should perhaps be understood as indicating obedience to God, that it is an expression of love for God, the love that is expected to result in the wish and the will to live in obedience to God. As we have already observed, at the beginning of the Isaiah book we have the demand for justice and righteousness, the words occurring as a pair. In both Deuteronomy 16:20 and 32:4 there appears to be portrayed the expression of the need for a real sense of fairness, equality and freedom for all the people, that there should prevail within the Israelite community acceptable, indeed correct, treatment of one person by another, in short that the spirit and the reality of social justice and righteousness should prevail throughout the land. This is what the Lord has demonstrated to his people in his treatment of them, and thus in both obedience to him and in imitation of him this is how the people of Israel should live in their communities.

However, all too often the words of the Hebrew prophets concern the *lack* of justice in the land—not infrequently expressed, again, as lack of justice and righteousness, as for example in Amos 5:7, "Ah, you that turn justice to wormwood, and bring righteousness to the ground!" See also Amos 5:24. In fact, the complaint of the Lord's prophet is what has happened in Israel is that justice has been turned into poison, and the fruit of righteousness into wormwood, which is to say that they have "gone bad" (Amos 6:12). Not dissimilar is the complaint that the prophet Micah makes, saying that should not the leaders of Israel "know justice," when in fact they have succeeded in giving the impression rather of their hating the good, loving the evil, allowing, as it were, the tearing of skin from off the people, the flesh off their bones. Which is perhaps to say that those who have been appointed to be the leaders of the people are themselves as good as living off the people (Mic 3:1–3)! Positively—and perhaps less gruesomely—the prophet proclaims,

> Come, let us go up to the mountain of the LORD,
> 　to the house of the God of Jacob;
> that he may teach us his ways,
> 　and that we may walk in his paths. (Mic 4:2)

Further, in particular with some of the Old Testament prophets we have stressed the great importance of worship being accompanied by the people living in justice and righteousness, which is to say that true worship of the Lord cannot come out of situations where there is no justice and righteousness. Indeed, what is being offered by those who are failing to live ethically good lives, is nothing short of an abomination to the Lord. Thus we read in the book of Isaiah:

> Trample my courts no more;
> bringing offerings is futile;
> 　incense is an abomination to me.
> New moon and sabbath and calling of convocation—
> 　I cannot endure solemn assemblies with iniquity.
> . . . .
> Wash yourselves; make yourselves clean;
> 　remove the evil of your doings
> 　from before my eyes;
> cease to do evil,
> 　learn to do good;
> seek justice,
> 　rescue the oppressed,
> defend the orphan,
> 　plead for the widow. (Isa 1:12b–13, 16–17)

Here, then, is another way in which parts of the Old Testament express the call to the people and leaders—and perhaps in particular the leaders and others who have special privileges and responsibilities—that they should live together in ethically good ways. These leaders shall live and rule with deep concerns that there will be justice and righteousness for all their peoples, that when those conditions do prevail for all in the land, they will indeed enjoy true life. That is, there shall be for all the people the gift of real and full life that all may truly enjoy living in equality and freedom.

But who might such leaders be? Deuteronomy 16:18–20 speaks of the call to appoint "judges and officials" throughout the Israelite tribes and towns who will render just and wise decisions for their peoples. Maybe it is these sorts of officials that we read about in such texts as Judg 8:16; Ruth 4:2; Job 29:7–8. Perhaps a part of the responsibilities of those who are called judges in the Old Testament book bearing that name involved "judging" the people and pronouncing judgments upon disputed matters, as well as the larger issue of defending the peoples from their enemies. Nevertheless, at a historically later time this "judging" became one of the major responsibilities of the king, as indeed we read in that so-called "Royal Psalm," Ps 72,

> May he judge your people with righteousness,
> and your poor with justice. (Ps 72:2)

And so also in that Isaianic vision of a coming ideal king set forth in Isa 9:2–7, where we read concerning this king of the line of David and his kingdom that, "He will establish and uphold it with justice and with righteousness from this time onwards and forevermore." (Isa 9:7)

The books of Chronicles seem to suggest that in the post-exilic community, when there was no Israelite king, the high priest took over the responsibility of being a supreme judge of the people (2 Chr 19:8). Nevertheless, whoever those in the Judean and Israelite societies called to be responsible for their peoples were, clearly the maintenance of justice and righteousness had a high importance. Leaders in age after age were appointed to exercise their best efforts in the attempt to maintain good ethical standards and to administer justice among and for all the people—and no doubt this especially on behalf of all those who were themselves neither powerful nor wealthy. And where perhaps was the model of such an attitude and approach, the ideal of perfection? Surely, in none other than the Lord God, who according to the prophet of Isa 40–55 says, "There is no other god besides me, a righteous God and a Savior; there is no one besides me." (Isa 45:21) For who in this regard can doubt this Lord? "Does God pervert justice? Or does the Almighty pervert the right?" (Job 8:3) Which appropriately leads us into considering another aspect of our appealing to the Old Testament for help in making our ethical decisions, that of Imitation of God, that is our seeking to act ethically in what we might call godly ways—in fact seeking to act in ways that imitate those of the Lord.

Imitation of God

In the Old Testament book of Leviticus, as we have already observed, we read about a particular word that is set forth as a command from the Lord to his people, namely, "You shall be holy, for I the LORD your God am holy." (Lev 19:2) And indeed this whole chapter of Leviticus is about the ethical life of God's people, the Israelites. When we are told here that the Lord is "holy" we may understand this as meaning that he is exalted, that he is awesome in power, that he is glorious in appearance, and that he has—and indeed exercises—a purity of character. It is with the last-named of these that we are at present concerned, in particular the talk here that as the Lord exercises a purity of character in his dealings with his people, so should his people seek to exercise the same in their dealings with one another. Yet the suggestion here is not that the people of Israel have to "make up" their "purity of character" but rather that they should seek in their dealings with one another to be *imitators* of the Lord. Thus, while any details are but sparingly given, we read that Enoch "walked with God" (Gen 5:22, 24) suggesting that there was indeed a closeness to God of the man Enoch whose life, it is perhaps suggesting, was one of some attempt at imitating the divine ways and actions. Further, and reverting to what was said above about Lev 19, we may observe that a series of situations is outlined where this "imitation" of the Lord's ways with his people may be worked out, lived out as it were, by the people in Israel in their dealing with one another. A real sense of reverence for parents (Lev 19:9); generous remembering of the poor in the gathering of the crops (19:9–10); fairness in judicial matters (19:15), and honesty in business dealings (19:35–36) are mentioned in this context.

Then in the book of Deuteronomy we find a further example of this "imitation of God," as for instance in the words, "Remember that you were a slave in the land of Egypt, and the LORD your God redeemed you; for this reason I lay this command upon you today." (Deut 15:15) Here are the people of Israel surely being called not to oppress other people, but rather to act in compassionate and delivering ways with them. In the same chapter of Deuteronomy there is the command that a released slave should go on his or her way having received from their master liberally from the flock, the threshing floor and the wine press, "thus giving to him some of the bounty with which the LORD has blessed you" (Deut 15:13–14). Further, in Exodus where we read about how we are to behave on the seventh day, that is we are to rest, this is to apply not just for the leaders of the community, but also for others of its members: "Six days you shall do your work, but on the seventh day you shall rest, so that your ox and your donkey may have relief, and your homeborn slave and the resident alien may be refreshed." (Exod 23:12) And this, of course, because God, according to the ancient story of the creation of the world, had worked on the six days and then rested on the seventh. Thus are his people called to be *imitators* of him in this regard. However, there are bounds in this matter, for while members of humanity are called to *imitate* God, they are not to seek to be *like* God. This of course we are told clearly in the story in Genesis 3 about not eating of that particular tree in the midst of the garden, "for God knows that when you eat of it your eyes will be opened, and you will be like God, knowing good and evil." (Gen 3:5) We are called to remember with humility who and what we are, humans who are called in their dealings and lives to be seeking to *imitate* God, yet in humility before him. Which appears to be what the prophet Isaiah called his people to do:

> For the vineyard of the LORD of hosts
>   is the house of Israel,
> and the people of Judah
>   are his pleasant planting;
> he expected justice,
>   but saw bloodshed;
> righteousness,
>   but heard a cry! (Isa 5:7)

That is, the people are called to live in the ways of justice, kindness, and humility—as indeed God himself in his dealings with them has demonstrated. Humanity's call is to seek to imitate God, while failure to seek to do so will inevitably be an aspect of human rebellion (Isa 30:9). And so also in other parts of the Old Testament. Thus Ps 81:13, for example, gives expression to a deep-seated wish of the Lord,

> O that my people would listen to me,
>   that Israel would walk in my ways!

while another psalmist expresses the desire that something of the divine integrity and uprightness might be made manifest in human life; that prayer be made that such integrity and uprightness might preserve a person while he waits for the Lord (Ps 25:21).

It does have to be said that this approach to ethics and ethical living, namely of our seeking to "imitate" God, is not particularly prominent in the Old Testament, certainly not being as frequently spoken of as the corresponding "imitation of Christ" theme is in the New Testament, or in the later Christian tradition. Yet it is there, and it emphasizes the fact that God in his dealings with his people does act in ethically good ways, and that so should his people in their lives on earth act in like manner. Further, it surely also does need to be said that there is something particularly attractive about this approach to ethical living presented to us in parts of the Old Testament. For we are not being called upon here merely to obey rules and regulations, nor are we being invited to live in certain ways and with certain standards so that thereby we shall gain a series of benefits and bonuses. Rather we are being called, invited, to *imitate* the Lord in his loving, caring, purposeful dealings with his people throughout the ages—and also with us. There is something of an inspirational aspect here rather than one of fulfilling a stated duty; that is, we are inspired, encouraged to be and to act in imitation of God, and so to grow and hopefully develop as servants of God, as with the passing of time and experiences we become the more faithful people of his in the world.

The Paradigmatic Approach

Although the title of this approach to Old Testament ethics may seem somewhat off-putting, it does perhaps offer some useful guidance for us. It is something by way of being what we perhaps understand as a development of the "imitation" of God spoken of above. What is intended by this so-called "paradigmatic approach" is that in the Bible we have certain materials giving us guidance for our decision-making about ethical matters, and that here in the Old Testament is a series of particular challenges to imitate the biblical principles in ways that are appropriate for our lives in the world of today. Here are, we may say, crucial words of old to which we seek to give application in another setting in a later and, most likely, greatly different age. Or to put the matter the other way around, we might say that this so-called paradigmatic approach should help us to go some way towards discovering the sort of conduct and attitudes God expects from his people *today*. That is, we have in the Bible material that gives something by way of "models" or "examples" of the sort of conducts that are perhaps either appropriate or inappropriate for us to adopt in our own contemporary situations, indeed as we seek to "imitate" the ways of God in our daily and earthly lives.

For example, that Old Testament law that a farmer was not to reap to the very edges of his field or to "over-gather" his produce, whether of corn or of olives (Lev 19:9–10; Deut 24:19–21), can be seen to have certain serious difficulties if applied literally in the modern world. And yet the basic principle behind this law is surely as relevant as ever, that we should today be seeking to make proper provision for the sharing of earth's resources with those who are poor and vulnerable. Another example might be concerning the Old Testament law of the Year of Jubilee (Lev 25:8–55). This decreed that any inequalities in the social order should be righted, yet we might not unreasonably feel that this also would be difficult to get onto the modern world's statute books. Still, the principle is surely again sound, namely that in our contemporary world we should seek to make proper and due provision in a spirit of compassion for those many, many people in the world who are poor, homeless, and whose lives are dominated by debts with little chance of being able to pay them.

The principle here is that we are not seeking to introduce slavishly the ancient laws into *direct* usage in a vastly changed world, but that we are trying to take with the utmost seriousness the *basic principles* that gave rise in the ancient times to these laws. That is, we are seeing the ancient ethical instructions as *paradigms,* as examples, patterns for new applications in our very changed world; alternatively expressed, we might say that in some of these ancient stories, laws, instructions there is given to us a theoretical framework for us to take and adopt, and apply to situations and conditions in the world of today.

In this "paradigmatic" approach to Old Testament ethical stories and teachings we are trying to take seriously the spirit of a number of ancient texts coming from very different times to our own, and at the same time accepting that we then have to make them relevant and applicable in the modern world. Thus we are able to transfer ethical values espoused in the ancient Old Testament documents to challenge us in our very different world. Naturally, this process of transformation will possibly involve us in deep and maybe difficult discussions, and very likely disagreements, and yet at the same time our discussions must not lead to such bland platitudes and generalizations that the challenge in the ancient word of scripture is maybe ignored for another generation.

Conclusions

If our search is for examples of human beings involved in a serious attempt to living a full and godly ethical life we have to admit that the Old Testament is in all probability not either our most immediate or our most useful guide. There is manifestly rather too much in these ancient documents which presents quite unethical ways of life, for example much detail about warfare, and about the seizure of land and the associated denial of those lands to other peoples, who often must have regarded them as belonging to themselves by their long-standing possession of them and living in them. There is further a good deal about vengeance on enemies, and a certain number of what are morally offensive passages and stories to us—see for example what is to be the fate of those who struck, cursed, or reviled their parents (Exod 21:15, 17).

Yet, as we have seen above there is set out in this same Old Testament a real and deep concern for people who have particular needs, that is, for the oppressed, the orphans, the widows and others—that those who have particular needs are neither forgotten nor deliberately ignored. Further, there is a real concern that in Israel justice and righteousness should prevail, and that those who have particular responsibilities in this regard should ensure that such matters are carried out. There is moreover the call to individuals and communities to imitate God in their lives and their dealings with others, and also for us to contemplate what have been called those paradigms of human lives lived in good and godly ways in days of old and how such examples of living might appropriately be applied to life in the twenty-first century.

From Texts to Spirituality

The subject of this chapter has aspects that call for vigilance, prayer, and action on the part of those who search for a biblically-based spirituality for their lives. All too easily we may dismiss consideration of the Old Testament being able to help us with our making ethical decisions as being made up of documents hardly appropriate or suitable to make such contributions to our Christian spirituality. As we have seen certain parts of these scriptures do set forth ways of life which Christians must judge to be unworthy and occasionally unacceptable for imitation in a later age. Yet that should neither blind us, nor dull our senses and sensibilities, to those parts of the Old Testament that *do* in fact have real contributions to make to the living of the Christian life, such as doing our part in ensuring a continuing of the giving of important places to the thinking and praying about—and wherever and whenever possible the working out of—justice and righteousness in the societies of which we are a part. These are not matters that have any great mention in the New Testament, for the reason that those documents are taken up with other more immediately urgent and important matters.

Yet the Old Testament lays before us fairly and squarely the responsibility never to forget or neglect those in our societies who are in need, nor forget our seeking to imitate God—however unworthily and even sinfully we may work that out in our own everyday lives. Further, we may appreciate the provision of that help which has been labelled the "paradigmatic," that it may indeed by way of some examples be of sundry helps to us in our attempt at the living of the ever more-godly life—both individually, and also indeed corporately. Surely also the attempt on our parts to *imitate* God is a very real—indeed possibly necessary—part of the search of those who seek to live out a contemporary Christian spirituality. One of the very great, and justifiably highly regarded, works written long ago was the advice of Thomas à Kempis in his *The Imitation of Christ*. Very early in this famous work we read, "For sure, when the day of judgment comes, inquiry will not be made of us what we have read, but what we have done, not how well we have spoken, but how piously we have lived." So too we may wish to say that to a certain extent there are various pieces of guidance in the Old Testament scriptures about our call to the imitation of God in the living out of our spirituality, and at the same time may wish that we be given the strength to live likewise.

It will surely help us in these difficult matters to hold onto something of those Old Testament visions of the ideal society, in which there is a full place for all the peoples. In the days of the Hebrew kingdoms the vision could be of the ideal king who would bring about such conditions, but now for so many of us who live in democracies the vision must of necessity apply both to those who vote and as well as those who rule:

> May he defend the cause of the poor of the people,
>   give deliverance to the needy,
>   and crush the oppressor. (Ps 72:4)

Further, the Old Testament presents us with a remarkable vision for all peoples in our own days:

> Hate evil and love good,
>   and establish justice in the gate . . . (Amos 5:15a)

Thus may that end-time vision in the book of Isaiah one day come truly and completely to fulfillment:

> On this mountain the LORD of hosts will make for all peoples
>   a feast of rich food, a feast of well-aged wines,
>   of rich food filled with marrow,
>   of well-aged wines strained clear. (Isa 25:6)

8

Life with a Future

Your dead shall live, their corpses shall rise.
O dwellers in the dust, awake and sing for joy! (Isa 26:19a)

WHAT HAS THE OLD Testament to say about the future, in particular about the future for those people who live in the world, and what perhaps is there on this subject for those who look to the Old Testament to guide and encourage, help and strengthen them in their ongoing lives of spirituality? We may conveniently consider this under three headings, namely, Hope for Individuals; Hope for the nation; and Hope for the World. And to the first of these we now turn.

Hope for Individuals

In the book of Proverbs we read, "wait for the LORD, and he will help you." (Prov 20:22) This is a word set in the context of a person wishing to retaliate against someone for an "evil" done to them by the other. There are, as we have seen, a large number of psalms in the Old Testament that concern the woes an individual is experiencing in their life, and similarly a smaller number about the sufferings of a whole community, even a whole nation. In the majority of these psalms there is a resolution of the problem, in which case the psalmist is clearly able to go away with a real feeling of satisfaction and new hope. Thus, for example, in Psalm 71—one of the Individual Lament psalms—right there at the beginning we have the psalmist saying that he is taking refuge in his Lord, asking God to be a "rock of refuge" for him, "a strong fortress," indeed speaking personally and in a deep spirit of faith "my rock and my fortress" (Ps 71:1–3). Yet our psalmist has much to say, indeed much that he wishes to pour out to God. Thus he goes on crying out to God about his problems and difficulties (verses 4–11), asking that God will not forsake him (verses 12–21). And indeed it does seem that God is believed to be with him, and that truly he does help him, and more that he will go on helping him, because by the end of the psalm, the psalmist has broken out into the notes of praise and thanksgiving (verses 22–24). So the psalmist says, perhaps better, proclaims,

> My lips will shout for joy
>   when I sing praises to you;
>   my soul also, which you have rescued.
> All day long my tongue will talk of your righteous help,
>   for those who tried to do me harm
>   have been put to shame, and disgraced. (Ps 71:23–24)

Further, in a not dissimilar style are a number of outpourings from the heart of the prophet Jeremiah, who in being called to the prophetical ministry had found depths of human enmity that gave him such great pain and suffering. This series of anguished yet prayerful outpourings of the suffering prophet to the Lord who has called him to this very ministry, and thus also to all this great suffering, are to be found in Jer 11:18–23; 12:1–6; 15:15–21; 17:14–18; 18:19–23; 20:7–18. It does have to be said that not all of these passages conclude with the note of praise for the Lord's deliverance of his suffering servant. Yet at times there *is* sounded the real note of hope in the prophet's final word. Thus there is the note of God's judgment upon the prophet's enemies in Jer 11:22–23, while in 15:21 we read what is a great expression of assurance for ongoing life,

> I will deliver you out of the hand of the wicked,
>   and redeem you from the grasp of the ruthless. (Jer 15:21; see
> also 17:18; 18:23)

The book called Ecclesiastes, or Qoheleth, speaks of a whole series of most mysterious things that happen in the world, not the least of these being the fact that the person and reality of God seem to this writer to be somewhat distant from his people. Thus the book ends with the words, "The end of the matter; all has been heard. Fear God, and keep his commandments; for that is the whole duty of everyone." (Eccl 12:13)

And certainly we search in vain in this book for a confident expression of hope for the future. Nor, thinking of the future, is there expressed in this work any possibility of a life after death in which there may be the expectation of peace and a peaceful rest. Such is the rather limited sense of hope in the composition of Qoheleth.

How different is the whole tone of the twenty-third psalm, which right from its opening word expresses an apparently boundless hope in the Lord, such hope that the psalmist asks what further needs he can possibly have, "The LORD is my shepherd, I shall not want."

The writer, the psalmist, goes on to speak of the Lord's care and loving provision for him being made manifest and practical in times of resting quietly in the peace of the Lord. This is illustrated in the language of lying in green pastures, being led by calm waters, being restored in life, and indeed of ever being led in right paths (Ps 23:1–3). Further, all this the Lord does in the way that he has always cared for his people, in the same way that he has a reputation for doing, that is "for his name's sake." (v. 3)

Then, what does the psalmist mean to indicate by the words translated in the NRSV "Even though I walk through the darkest valley"? (v. 4) For as the translators of that English version make clear in their footnote it could also be rendered, "Even though I walk through the valley of the shadow of death." The word used could also be intended to speak of the actual death of a person, in which case there is expressed the belief of the psalmist—and the intended assurance for the readers and the hearers of this psalm—that with God there is the promise of life after death, eternal life. Alternatively, it could be that the word "death" is being used to express the sense of deepest darkness ("dead dark, deathly darkness"), that is the worst case scenario for *this* earthly life. Or equally, it could be that the psalmist wishes in his psalm to give expression to *both* of these possibilities, *both* the Lord's presence with a person in the worst experiences of life on earth, *and also* his divine presence in actual death and in a good and blessed future beyond that. Perhaps even, it could be that the psalmist wished to cover *both* of these situations. That is, the psalmist had this abounding confidence that results in his composing his psalm in a spirit of joyful proclamation, which lays such emphasis on the powerful and strengthening presence of the Lord with him, wherever he is, in life or even maybe in death. For indeed, "I fear no evil; for you are with me; your rod and your staff—they comfort me." (Ps 23:4)

Nevertheless, whatever may be those ongoing, and surely reasonable, doubts we may have about just what this psalmist wishes to convey to us of his beliefs concerning the fact, the sheer reality of human death, it has to be said that his psalm is full of confident expectations. He is sure of the Lord's loving provisions for him, and that the divine goodness and mercy will follow him all the days of his life, so that he will indeed be able to—and will indeed wish to—live in fellowship with the Lord his "whole life long." (Ps 23:5–6) Further, it may even be that while this is a faith to be lived out in the world, it is yet also about matters that are beyond the limits of merely material life. Further, we could say that these are indeed some human probings and enquiries in a deep spirit of faith into the realms of the spiritual life.

We may consider other possible texts from the Old Testament that seem to be suggesting the power of the Lord over death, and an associated belief in the reality of life after death, and first we go to Ps 73, a psalm we have earlier considered. It begins with the recital of a problem the particular psalmist here clearly had, namely why is it, and how can it be, that certain wicked people seem to be doing so well for themselves in their earthly lives? How can it be that this is allowed by God to take place? Thus this psalmist cries out to God about the prosperity of certain wicked people he has observed, in particular in vv. 4–9. But then for this psalmist what appears to be a further thought is spoken of concerning his being remarkably safe and fortunate, for not only was he with God continually, and that God was ever with him here on earth, but also that this could go on, in fact applying also to life after death. Thus the psalmist speaks of the Lord guiding him with his counsel, and further that he, the Lord, will receive the psalmist "with honor" (v. 24). Now the word translated "with honor" in verse 24, could also be read as indicating "to glory," and it may be that it was intended to indicate the sense of a belief in life after death in the very presence and the loving care of the Lord. This, it needs to be said, may not have been what the psalmist intended, but equally it could be.

Another of the psalms, Psalm 49, is perhaps somewhat clearer in this matter of a belief in life after death, for it reads,

> But God will ransom my soul from the power of Sheol,
> for he will receive me. (Ps 49:15)

Sheol for the Old Testament is the setting for that somewhat shadowy existence to which people are believed to go after their earthly death; it is not the life of heaven, nor is it eternal life. However, in Ps 49:15 there is also the thought expressed in the words, "for he will receive me"—which could have been translated "for he will take me"—coming from a Hebrew verb that also occurs in Gen 5:24, "Enoch walked with God; then he was no more because God took him." We understand this as expressing something in the nature of an existence in the fellowship of God *after* human life was over. Perhaps indeed here the psalmist was thinking about a life after death, though no details are given.

However, on this subject the language and the talk in Daniel chapter 12 are surely both more confident and clearer to us about intended meaning than are Pss 73 and 49:

> At that time Michael, the great prince, the protector of your people, shall arise. There shall be a time of anguish, such as has never occurred since nations first came into existence. But at that time your people shall be delivered, everyone who is found written in the book. Many of those who sleep in the dust of the earth shall awake, some to everlasting life, and some to shame and everlasting contempt. Those who are wise shall shine like the brightness of the sky, and those who lead many to righteousness, like the stars forever and ever. (Dan 12:1–3)

Here surely is a real expression of hope for God's faithful people after death. No details are given, but here as one scholar put it, there is a "breaking the silence of the grave and affirming the communion of saints as part of the purposes of God."

Nor in this regard should we neglect Isa 26:19, for this verse also surely speaks of the hope of new life. While the preceding verses 17 and 18 are about aspects of the futility of parts of human life, likening them to the agonies of a woman in childbirth who then gives birth to no more than wind, we have in the following verse a truly confident word coming from the vision the writer has been vouchsafed,

> Your dead shall live, their corpses shall rise,
>   O dwellers in the dust, awake and sing for joy!
> For your dew is a radiant dew,
>   and the earth will give birth to those long dead. (Isa 26:19)

Thus are some of the Old Testament's expressions of the hope that people may have of the love of God for their individual lives, and something too of the somewhat cautious moves we find in these documents towards the belief in a life beyond death. Such possible, and perhaps tentative, beginnings of these beliefs we can observe being further developed in the Intertestamental period (that is between the Old and New Testament periods) and coming to a real fullness of belief in the New Testament. Yet here in the Old Testament, as we have seen, we do have some witnesses to a growing and developing belief that there are possibilities for the life of spirituality of earthly peoples to be found afresh—and surely in a series of deeper experiences of divine care, God's presence with us in a new way—in a life after death. And if we are talking about a life after earthly death, then that must presumably—that is as far as we can know on this side of things—be in the nature of a spiritual life.

Hope for the Nation

So much then for the hope which is given expression in the Old Testament for individuals, but what of the hope for the future of the nation, the whole people? In the last chapter of the book of the prophet Amos there is a boldly portrayed confidence that at some time in the future the prospects for the Israelite nation are indeed good. Whether or not this passage really comes from Amos has long been questioned, for the reason that so much else in this book is a somewhat gloomy prediction of the woes that are inevitably coming upon a sinful people as a result of their self-centered and foolish life styles, and their apparent neglect of God and his commands and desires. Yet *someone* has written what we have in Amos 9:11–14, and those words, either sooner or later, came to be part of what finally was incorporated into the Hebrew Bible, our Old Testament, and can thus surely be considered in this study. The heart of this passage reads as follows:

> The time is surely coming, says the LORD,
> when the one who plows shall overtake the one who reaps,
> and the treader of grapes the one who sows the seed;
> the mountains shall drip sweet wine,
> and all the hills shall flow with it.
> I will restore the fortunes of my people Israel,
> and they shall rebuild the ruined cities and inhabit them;
> they shall plant vineyards and drink their wine,
> and they shall make gardens and eat their fruit.
> I will plant them upon their land,
> and they shall never again be plucked up
> out of the land that I have given them, says the LORD your God.
> (Amos 9:13–15)

All this is a thoroughly this-worldly vision of a time of new beginnings, when there will be, according to these promises, so many good things happening for the people of Israel in the worldly setting of life in their promised land. A much more detailed vision of a good and beneficial future for the people of Israel is to be found in chs 40–55 of the book of Isaiah, the prophecies of the so-called Second Isaiah. These chapters seem to have come from the days when many of the people of Israel were in exile in Babylon, but the change of kingship there made it, from a political point of view, possible for many of the exiles to return to their own homelands. For Cyrus the Persian (see Isa 44:28; 45:1) had reasons of his own for letting exiles from other lands return to their homelands, on condition that they acknowledged his rule over them, that they paid their taxes to the Persians, and that they prayed to their own God for him, their ruler, Cyrus. Thus a great and thrilling new exodus is portrayed as about to take place (see Isa 40:3–11; 43:14–21).

Yet, while this at one level may be understood as a militaristic venture into the unknown, there are other notes distinctly sounded in these chapters, for amongst the joyful passages in Isa 40–55, there are other matters presented, the main one surely being the four passages about a servant, Isa 42:1–4; 49:1–6; 50:4–9; 52:13—53:12, which over the years and decades have been much-discussed—and indeed in this present work we have considered them a number of times—in particular as to who the servant is. A wide range of views has been presented, and the approach I take, and which is adopted in this work, is that the "servant" portrayed in these passages is the people of Israel themselves as they prepare to undertake the journey back to their own land, and thus make their exit from the land of exile. That is, these people are being called not to go back home as conquering heroes, but rather as servants, those who will serve others, those even who may have to give their lives in service to other people. There is something here that is surely deeply spiritual about this new life of these descendants of the Israelites of old, for they are being warned that they will not live and succeed in a worldly sense of those terms, but as servants of the Lord, and of other people. They will thus not display a *worldly* picture of either strength or success, but they will be possessed of a *spiritual* sense of direction, inner-strength, and purpose in their lives, above all being servants of God, of one another, and of others.

Another of the prophetic visions that come out of the years of exile is that of the prophet Jeremiah, who though himself not in exilic Babylon, proclaimed the coming of a new relationship between God and his people, a relationship that is portrayed as being much deeper and inward than the equivalent earlier one. Thus we read,

> But this is the covenant that I will make with the house of Israel after those days, says the LORD: I will put my law within them, and I will write it on their hearts; and I will be their God, and they shall be my people. No longer shall they teach one another, or say to each other, "Know the LORD," for they shall all know me, from the least of them to the greatest, says the LORD; for I will forgive their iniquity, and remember their sin no more. (Jer 31:33–34)

What is being indicated here? It is something in the nature of a new start for God's people, for those people who in the past have failed to maintain their faithfulness to the Lord. Yet even more than a renewed start, it is perhaps rather nothing less than a new *relationship*. For here is the assurance that now the people, forgiven their sins of the past, can enter into a new, and indeed closer, relationship with the Lord than they had known hitherto, this being indicated by the expression concerning the Lord putting his law within his peoples' hearts. That is, what in past times was intended to be the teaching and instructional ministry of parents and of the priests—and maybe also at times that of the Levites too—has become something done *personally* by God for each of his people directly. Here is portrayed the inner life of an individual person being divinely given something in the nature of a supernatural gift. This is given some added emphasis through the use of the Hebrew verb "know" in Jer 31:34 concerning the people knowing the Lord, which carries a range of meanings not only "knowing" through having knowledge, but also expressing the fact of having a deep and close relationship with another—whether that be with a spouse or another family member, or whether it is with none other than the Lord God. Such must surely represent some of the import of the promise expressed in Jer 31:34 about God's people "knowing" the Lord, that is, they have what is indeed a close and deep relationship with their holy and divine Lord, what we might understand as being in the nature of a spiritual relationship with the Lord. In the extended quotation in the New Testament Letter to the Hebrews 8:8–12 we have the application of the promise expressed in Jer 31:31–34 to the new divine dispensation in the Christian Church in lives lived in the faith of the Lord Jesus.

Something also in the Old Testament that speaks of a future hope for the nation of the people of Israel is given expression in the book of Ezekiel in the vision of the new temple in the long section Ezek 40:1—48:22. Indeed, the city in which this new temple stands will be called "The LORD is There" (Ezek 48:35), and the vision is given of a river flowing from below its threshold out into the surrounding countryside, thus enabling a flourishing of trees on both of its banks providing food for the people. Thus,

> On the banks, on both sides of the river, there will grow all kinds of trees for food. Their leaves will not wither nor their fruit fail, but they will bear fresh fruit every month, because the water for them flows from the sanctuary. Their fruit will be for food, and their leaves for healing. (Ezek 47:12)

Meanwhile, and totally unsurprisingly, there is in this temple and all it stands for, real provision for the interior lives of the people, what we would refer to as their spiritual lives. For in this elaborate vision of a new Jerusalem temple the prophet speaks of the presence of the Lord in the temple and thereby with his people:

> As the glory of the LORD entered the temple by the gate facing
> east, the spirit lifted me up, and brought me into the inner court;
> and the glory of the LORD filled the temple. While the man was
> standing beside me, I heard someone speaking to me out of the
> temple. He said to me: Mortal, this is the place of my throne and
> the place for the soles of my feet, where I will reside among the
> people of Israel forever. (Ezek 43:4–7a)

Thus here and elsewhere are expressions of hope for the future of the
Israelite nation, and in particular of the hope of a deeper inward, surely
spiritual, notion of the relationship between the Lord and his people.

Hope for the World

The biblical expressions of hope for the world are generally to be found in
that type of biblical material we call "apocalyptic," a word from the Greek
meaning "revelation" or "disclosure," a word we find at the beginning of the
New Testament book of Revelation, "The revelation of Jesus Christ, which
God gave him to show his servants what must soon take place . . ." (Rev
1:1). In the biblical apocalypses there are visions, and a deal of symbolism
is employed, sometimes a human seer and maybe also an otherworldly
mediator are spoken of. Moreover, frequently otherworldly journeys, and
events are portrayed as taking place in the cosmic world. God is pictured as
transcendent, and thus there are angels who mediate between him and his
people of earth. Further, these writings seem to come out of times of human
suffering in the world, and they seek to say something about the Lord's apparent purposes, and his activity—or seeming inactivity—in the world. We
surely glimpse something of these features in a part of the New Testament
book of Revelation, where we are told,

> Then I saw a new heaven and a new earth; for the first heaven
> and the first earth had passed away, and the sea was no more.
> And I saw the holy city, the new Jerusalem, coming down out of
> heaven from God, prepared as a bride adorned for her husband.
> (Rev 21:1–2)

One of the major pieces of apocalyptic in the Old Testament is in the
book of Daniel chs 7–12. These chapters are about the future, and in particular they set forth a series of visions about what God himself in direct
and decisive intervention will do to transform the troubled earthly world.
There are four visions found in chs 7, 8, 9, and 10–12, each of them speaking
of the rise and then later dramatic fall of a series of earthly kingdoms, and

eventually of the faithful ones of earth being saved. In the final chapter of the book we read of the arrival of Michael, the great prince, the protector of God's people, and out of a time of anguish there will be both judgment and also salvation. Thus for example we read in Dan 12:

> At that time Michael, the great prince, the protector of your people, shall arise. There shall be a time of anguish, such as has never occurred since nations first came into existence. But at that time your people shall be delivered, everyone who is found written in the book. Many of those who sleep in the dust of the earth shall awake, some to everlasting life, and some to shame and everlasting contempt. Those who are wise shall shine like the brightness of the sky, and those who lead many to righteousness, like the stars forever and ever. (Dan 12:1–3)

And yet alongside this great and reassuring vision there is the realistic appraisal of the state of the world and the apparent continuation in the meantime of more evil lives and deeds:

> But you, Daniel, keep the words secret and the book sealed until the time of the end. Many shall be running back and forth, and evil shall increase. (Dan 12:4)

While there may be only these two biblical works, Daniel and Revelation, that are what scholars have called apocalyptic works, there are also parts of books that while they may not be fully apocalyptic, yet have features of this type of biblical literature. An example of this, what has been called proto-apocalyptic—that is written material on the way, so to speak, to becoming fully apocalyptic—occurs in the book of Isaiah, in the section chs 24–27. Within this part of the Isaiah book we find a distinct emphasis about the Lord's work of judgment upon the earth, as for example in Isa 24:1, "Now the Lord is about to lay waste the earth and make it desolate . . ." And a little later,

> The earth dries up and withers,
> the world languishes and withers;
> the heavens languish together with the earth. (Isa 24:4)

There is nothing here as yet about the humans and their actions and lives, and the possibility of good things happening for those who have sought to remain faithful to the Lord. That is until we come to ch 25, where we read:

> On this mountain the Lord of hosts will make for all peoples
> a feast of rich food, a feast of well-aged wines,

of rich food filled with marrow, of well-aged wines strained clear.
And he will destroy on this mountain
the shroud that is cast over all peoples,
the sheet that is spread over all nations;
he will swallow up death forever.
Then the LORD God will wipe away the tears from all faces,
and the disgrace of his people he will take away from all the earth,
for the LORD has spoken.
It will be said on that day,
Lo, this is our God; we have waited for him, so that he might save us.
This is the LORD for whom we have waited;
let us be glad and rejoice in his salvation. (Isa 25:6–9)

At the beginning of Isa 26 is the call to people to put their trust in the Lord, for there they will find they have "an everlasting rock", which will give them a real sense of peace. (Isa 26:3–4) In the preceding chapter is the gift of food—and rich, good food and drink! (25:6)—that is promised by the Lord of hosts for all peoples. Indeed, these gifts appear clearly to be for all people, there is nothing here about them only being available for certain peoples who have lived in particularly good ways, ways that have been well-pleasing to the Lord. Rather, these great gifts are apparently for everyone, and we should surely take note of the emphasis here about "all people." Further, death will be wiped out, along with tears, and any feelings of disgrace (25:8). Here indeed is the salvation for which so many people have waited. Thus can be changed that "shroud," that "sheet" of v. 7—perhaps intended to indicate a veil for a time of mourning?—for the spirit of celebration and rejoicing. For such will be, we are told, for *all peoples.*

Then in the following chapter in the book of Isaiah is the talk of an "improved" vineyard, one that will call for singing about, one over which the Lord will be the keeper and which he will constantly tend, guarding it night and day with a great readiness to fight the thorns and briers (Isa 27:2–5). We can hardly help but be reminded of the vineyard talk much earlier in the book of Isaiah (Isa 5:1–7). Yet, of course, neither of these passages are really about vineyards; rather, the ch 5 vineyard-talk is intended to speak about and illustrate the sinfulness and irresponsible stewardship of the people of Israel at an earlier moment in their history, while the ch 27 one is about a future of great divine mercies and blessings to be set before the people of Israel—and in fact thereby for none other than the people of the whole world. Thus we read,

On that day:
A pleasant vineyard, sing about it!

> I, the LORD, am its keeper,
>   every moment I water it.
> I guard it night and day
>   so that no one can harm it;
>   I have no wrath.
> If it gives me thorns and briers,
>   I will march to battle against it,
>   I will burn it up.
> Or else let it cling to me for protection,
>   let it make peace with me,
>   let it make peace with me.
> In days to come Jacob shall take root,
>   Israel shall blossom and put forth shoots,
>   and fill the whole world with fruit. (Isa 27:2–6)

Thus is promised a whole world filled with fruit (v. 6), with peace (v. 5), and with divine protection (v. 3). Indeed, a remarkable picture of a truly pleasant vineyard to sing about! Which is to say, what very great and remarkable hope there is so boldly and confidently being given here for nothing less than the whole world. The fact that there is now a pleasant vineyard speaks of a promised deep transformation both of what is growing in the land and that will be of benefit for the population, but also of the good and pleasing appearance of this richly producing area. Moreover this vineyard is under divine care and protection, emphasis being given to the necessary tasks and duties that will be carried out by none other than the Lord himself—keeping it, watering it, guarding it night and day so that there can be no fear from the presence and activities of any who may make trouble. Further, the appearance of any thorns and briers will attract the divine rescue. This will indeed be a vineyard to sing joyfully about; about the former vineyard there was a divine love-song (Isa 5:1), but surely this is indeed a very different composition extolling the latter vineyard (Isa 27:2)! Further, the peace being spoken about would seem to be between the latter vineyard and the Lord: that is, whereas in the case of the former, the Lord came and destroyed it, for indeed it had become useless (Isa 5:3–6), now there will be peace between the latter vineyard and the Lord God.

There is one further emphasis presented in the book of Isaiah that we should consider in this present context. As we have already observed there is introduced in chapters 40–55 of the book of Isaiah the thought of a servant of the Lord, spoken about in Isa 42:1–4; 49:1–6; 50:4–9; 52:13–53:12 which, I have suggested above, refers to the people of Israel being called to live as servants of the Lord. The particular servant-calling spoken of in the Isa 49:1–6 passage concerns mission to the nations, for the Lord's concern is that the divine light and the gift of salvation may go far beyond the bounds of the lands of the Israelite people, and may be offered to the peoples of other lands and other nations. Thus, we read, concerning the Lord's wish as to his servant's mission,

> He says,
> "It is too light a thing that you should be my servant
>   to raise up the tribes of Jacob
>   and to restore the survivors of Israel;
> I will give you as a light to the nations,
>   that my salvation may reach to the end of the earth." (Isa 49:6)

Here is the striking statement that the Lord wishes to become as light of the nations, in order that his saving ministry may be felt and experienced in lands beyond Israel and Judah, in fact throughout the world—that is the world as envisaged by the Old Testament writers. It is as one scholar has expressed it, "nothing other than the Torah [Law] that has been given to Moses on Sinai, but that is now valid for the world. This is the 'greater' message. It is a message for the future."

From Texts to Spirituality

Our considerations in this chapter have taken us through a broad swath of the ancient world as seen and understood by ancient Israelite people as we have asked what the Old Testament has to say about life under God in future times. It has been observed that there is expressed within the pages of the Hebrew Bible a real concern to proclaim a message for the futures of individual peoples, for the people of the Israelite nation, and in fact further for the peoples of the whole wider world. That is to say, there is in the Old Testament a real expression of the concerns and purposes of God with individual people, with nationalism, and even with universalism.

It is not that this is anything very surprising. After all, the Old Testament begins with a theological account of the beginning time when God is portrayed as having created the heavens and the earth (Gen 1:1—2:25). Yet all too soon one of the men of the earth had for his own safety to flee to another land, namely Cain, son of Adam and Eve who, having killed his brother Abel, fled to and settled in the land of Nod, which we are told was east of Eden (Gen 4:16). Further, later generations of the descendants of Adam and Eve are portrayed as travelling to other countries, perhaps above all Abraham. In the fullness of time Egypt would very much come into the Old Testament's historical frame and its ongoing story, and later other, and growing, nations, those of the Assyrians, Babylonians, Persians, Greeks and Romans. And all these—some being spoken of openly while others less specifically—have a place in the Old Testament records, in as we have observed, various of the books and documents, thus highlighting the Lord's concern for these extra-Israelite areas and peoples.

Any spirituality which seeks guidance and content from the Old Testament must surely have these various foci in mind, especially those three we have considered in this chapter: individual people, the Israelites' own nation, and also the whole world. For our documents speak of life, and hope, and the search for a secure and meaningful future for all three of these groupings, which may be said to be illustrated by quotations from two of the psalms, namely Pss 80:3, 7, 19 and 67:1–7:

> Restore us, O God;
>> let your face shine, that we may be saved.
>
> Restore us, O God of hosts;
>> let your face shine, that we may be saved.
>
> Restore us, O LORD God of hosts;
>> let your face shine, that we may be saved. (Ps 80:3, 7, 19)

> May God be gracious to us and bless us
>> and make his face to shine upon us,
>> that your way may be known upon earth,
>> your saving power among all nations.
> Let the peoples praise you, O God;
>> let all the peoples praise you.
> Let the nations be glad and sing for joy,
>> for you judge the peoples with equity
>> and guide the nations upon earth.
> Let the peoples praise you, O God;
>> let all the peoples praise you.
> The earth has yielded its increase;
>> God, our God, has blessed us.
> May God continue to bless us;
>> let all the ends of the earth revere him. (Ps 67:1–7)

Thus does the Old Testament speak of a hope of and belief in a future not only for individual people, but also for the particular Israelite nation, and yet further for the whole world. While with any future hope for an individual nation, and also that of the whole world, there will be the reality of the earthly settings and conditions for those involved—as well as, surely, spiritual possibilities. But that future hope for individual people is singularly focussed upon a spiritual setting, and as far as we know on this side of things must inevitably be about a future *spiritual* existence and life. Perhaps John Donne (1572–1631) has expressed as much of the spirituality of this new and renewed life as can be grasped here on earth when he said in a sermon:

> And into that gate they shall enter, and in that house they shall dwell, where there shall be no Cloud nor Sun, no darkenesse nor dazling, but one equall light, no noyse nor silence, but one equall musick, no fears nor hopes, but one equal possession, no foes nor friends, but one equall communion and Identity, no ends nor beginnings, but one equall eternity.

That, of course, was to be revealed in considerably later times than those from which our Old Testament texts come, and yet perhaps there is within those ancient texts a certain developing sense of belief about a future hope for the world, but also for the nation, and in particular for individual people.

9

The Old Testament
and Christian Spirituality

Then God said, "Let us make humankind in our image, according to our likeness" (Gen 1:26a)

WHAT IS THERE IN the Old Testament, the Hebrew Bible, on our subject of
spirituality which we maybe do not find in other parts of the scriptures?
Although we can well understand that Christians would expect in a biblical
search to go in the first place to the New Testament, yet at the same time they
may well ask what perhaps there is further in the Old Testament, which after
all makes up the largest part of the Jewish/Christian Bible. Which is perhaps
to pose the question, what have we discovered in the preceding chapters of
this present work? What useful conclusions have we harvested concerning
matters of spirituality, some conclusions that could usefully contribute to
the spiritual lives of others and ourselves?

We may begin by considering the matter of the time span of the
documents that make up the Old Testament, this being approached in
two senses. For many of us these days we would not profess to know from
which times, even ages, some of the contributions in these scriptures come.
While some of the Old Testament books may profess to be speaking about
times of long, long ago, they may in fact perhaps be documents that do not
come from such early times, and nor do they perhaps accurately represent
matters historical. Rather, in them the theological matters predominate.
Nevertheless, such materials may well have significant, even important,
contributions—from some particular age or other—to make about Israelite

faith. Such contributions may aid us in our study of, and perhaps also in our search for, a Christian spirituality for our lives, both individual and also corporate, for today.

However, by the time we come to the reign of king David in Jerusalem—that is from around one thousand years BCE—we are reading documents and records that could well represent reasonably accurate matters historical—though of course we have to allow for the particular approaches of various authors, their individual concerns and emphases, and for the possibilities that writing at a later time they felt a need to emphasize certain happenings, acts, decisions so as to better explain various later events and happenings.

Nevertheless, there is a remarkable time span from around 1,000 BCE to the time of the last compositions of documents that make up what we know as the Old Testament, and within a number of parts of the Old Testament we do observe a series of changes of emphases, some variations in approach to sundry matters. Further, one of the very great changes that is to be observed taking place in this whole time span comes out of the whole experience of the exile in Babylon and elsewhere for a number, perhaps a significant number, of the Israelite peoples. Later, for some of those exiles there was the further experience of returning to their own lands, and under what they inevitably experienced as a series of changed situations, where they sought to re-establish their communal life and worship.

It would seem that there is a sense in which our present book of Isaiah, whatever we think about its authorship, spans the times before, during, and after the exile. Certainly, some of the earlier chapters clearly seem to be making reference to eighth century BCE issues, speaking of kings whose activities and responsibilities were, in Israelite and Judean historical terms, in pre-exilic times and whose reigns coincided with those of kings of other countries and nations of those times. Later, in the middle parts of the Isaiah book we hear of the political and military rule of the Persian man, Cyrus, over a wide range of lands and peoples. Then further in chs 56–66 of Isaiah we are given the clear impression that the historical scenario is that of the as-yet unrebuilt Jerusalem temple to which at least some of the one-time exiles have come back. Moreover, whereas in some earlier times, now long-past, certain regulations in the book of Leviticus make it clear that those who served as priests had to be of the lineage of Aaron, now in this later time not only will the temple be a house, a sanctuary for *all* peoples (Isa 56:6–7), but also there will be strangers, that is presumably people of other nationalities and peoples, who will be called "priests of the LORD . . . ministers of our God" (Isa 61:6).

This is but one example of a changed, and perhaps also as it was being written still changing, situation that we encounter in our reading and study of the Old Testament. Our sources for the whole composition of the Hebrew Bible cover times when the people of God experienced freedom in their national lives, times when they were the less free, times too of exile away from their own homeland, and constrained by overlords. By comparison the time scale of the New Testament is short indeed, though of course we do encounter there a changed situation in its last book, that of Revelation. Yet the New Testament's central and crucial emphasis and concern is upon the great new event of the coming of Christ, and those documents are in the main concerned with the story, and the significance, of the birth, life, death, and resurrection of Jesus—and further about his sending out of his disciples and thereby laying the foundations of the new church. Thus here also is teaching about the life and the role of that infant church. That is to say, the New Testament documents are of a very different nature from those of the Old Testament, those of the New are neither so varied in their content, nor covering so many periods of earthly history, as are those of the Old.

The Old Testament as it is presented to us sets forth a very large canvas of historical settings—what we might imagine covering an extended horizontal time line. Along that line we perceive a variety of responses to changing situations. Thus among the Old Testament documents, covering as they do so much time, along with many issues and experiences, we are hardly surprised to find a number of documents and parts of documents that deal with those complex issues of suffering, which may even have been intended to help their readers and hearers to deal with their latter-day experiences of suffering. If these people really are in the care and keeping of the Lord God, how can it be that they must go through so many times of suffering and loss? Surely, these documents may help their latter-day readers—perhaps themselves going through times of change—to find help in *their* search for a Christian spirituality, whether here there is an uncomfortable or whether a comforting response.

Another on-going experience that the Old Testament speaks about concerns what ethical ways the people of God are called upon to adopt, this again being an issue which it is surely important for attention by those who seek to live out their spirituality in church and world relationships and communities. As we have already observed there are some problems for us with various of the ethical stances spoken about in the Old Testament, and yet at other times and in other parts of these scriptures there are examples of how we *should* live, act, behave in this situation or that. What is right and what is wrong for these people spoken about in the Old Testament texts, and what is right and what is wrong for us individuals, communities, nations in this or that setting in so much later times? There are set out briefly in the preceding study some examples illustrating how perhaps parts of the Old Testament might be turned to for help. For as we have seen there are some situations in which our ethical decision-making might be helped by such considerations as how we should seek to imitate God; by considering some paradigms of good behavior we might seek to emulate; by asking what might be done—and in particular what we might do—to aid the search for, and the associated bringing about, of justice and righteousness in our contemporary world. Certainly this is a topic that cries out for serious attention on the part of those who live aware of the spiritual dimensions of earthly existence. Surely, how many remarkable stories and rich teachings are written about here in the Old Testament scriptures that speak of the place of the human beings in the world, and in particular of the spiritual dimensions of their lives. Yet at the same time, we surely have to acknowledge that parts of the Old Testament do present words and actions that are of less help to us—and that truly there are individuals and groups whose portrayed standards and morals can hardly be accepted today.

Yet there are other aspects of life about which the Old Testament speaks to us. If with matters of suffering we may be in the symbolic depths, we may now, further to our earlier tracing of that imaginary horizontal line, that time line, imagine now that we are also tracing an imaginary vertical line. This is to represent something of the heights and depths of human experiences. First then, let us consider the top point of it where we may feel that it is appropriate to give priority to two subjects, those of creation and worship.

On the subject of creation, the Old Testament has two "accounts" of this, both of them being found in the very opening pages of both the Jewish and the Christian Bibles. John Calvin in his commentary on the book of Genesis begins his work by saying,

> Since the infinite wisdom of God is displayed in the admirable structure of heaven and earth, it is absolutely impossible to unfold The History of the Creation of the World in terms equal to its dignity. For while the measure of our capacity is too contracted to comprehend things of such magnitude, our tongue is equally incapable of giving a full and substantial account of them.

For there *is* surely a real note of wonder, the expression of a profound sense of awe, on the part of both the two authors of these accounts. In the first we have the solemn words, "In the beginning when God created the heavens and the earth . . . ." and very near the end we have "God saw everything that he had made, and indeed, it was very good. And there was evening and there was morning, the sixth day." (Gen 1:1, 31) Here indeed was the creation, the gift of a good dwelling-place for the people of earth. Further, it is then those people whose creation is very much the subject of the second account of the Lord's work of creation (Gen 2:4b-25), where we read towards its close,

> Then the LORD God formed man from the dust of the ground,
> and breathed into his nostrils the breath of life; and the man
> become a living being. (Gen 2:7)

And this sense of wonder finds remarkable expression in the nineteenth Psalm:

> The heavens are telling the glory of God;
> and the firmament proclaims his handiwork.
> Day to day pours forth speech,
> and night to night declares knowledge.
> There is no speech, nor are there words;
> their voice is not heard;
> yet their voice goes out through all the earth,
> and their words to the end of the world. (Ps 19:1–4)

It is truly a most particular part of the divine creation of the world that is portrayed in these words as being those of the human beings; indeed this is the sole theme in the second of these accounts (Gen 2:4b-25). Then also there is Ps 8 calling for comment, for this hymn of praise emphasizes in a remarkable way more about that most-exalted place accorded the human beings in the world. It speaks in particular of the close relationship of the humans with the Lord God:

> When I look at your heavens, the work of your fingers,
> the moon and the stars that you have established;
> what are human beings that you are mindful of them,
> mortals that you care for them?
> Yet you have made them a little lower than God,
> and crowned them with glory and honor.
> You have given them dominion over the works of your hands;
> you have put all things under their feet,
> all sheep and oxen,
> and also the beasts of the field,
> the birds of the air, and the fish of the sea,
> whatever passes along the paths of the seas.
> O LORD, our Sovereign,

how majestic is your name in all the earth! (Ps 8:3–9)

Then it is in the book of Exodus that we read of a pronounced emphasis upon the gracious divine provision for the people of Israel, who find themselves in a time and place of demanding existence under the harsh rule of the Pharaoh in Egypt, being expected to serve as laborers in his building schemes. The Israelite people's cries of distress and anguish are portrayed as being heard by the Lord God, who with the human effort and work of Moses brings his people out of the land of slavery, across the sea, and into the desert, eventually coming to the foot of Mount Horeb/Sinai (Exod 1:1— 18:27). Much then happens at this desert-stage on the Israelites' journey, where they are encamped at the foot of the holy mountain. For there on the mountain Moses receives the tablets of the law—what we know as the Ten Commandments—and God makes a gracious covenant agreement with the people, which in essentials is about the Lord being God to these people, while they obeying his commands become his "priestly kingdom," his "holy nation." Thus God is portrayed as speaking, and instructing Moses as to what he is to say to the whole people of Israel:

> Now therefore, if you obey my voice and keep my covenant, you shall be my treasured possession out of all the peoples. Indeed, the whole earth is mine, but you shall be for me a priestly kingdom and a holy nation. These are the words that you shall speak to the Israelites. (Exod 19:5–6)

So the people of Israel come into covenant relationship with the Lord. We then go on to read in the book of Exodus account detailed instructions about how these people will be led on through the desert towards the promised land, how they are to live their lives, how they are to worship, and what they should build for their religious sanctuaries—presumably when they eventually cross over into the promised land.

The crucial thing for us to note is surely that this place, at the foot of Mount Horeb/Sinai, is the place of covenant making, that is the covenant that God makes with his people Israel, the heart of which is quoted above, and the whole concept of which we have considered in some detail in ch 2 above. And yet, of course, these covenant words in Exod 19 are not the end of the matter, for it is as if our Old Testament theologians/writers revisit them from time to time, thus while at one moment this prophet will see them in a new light, or that prophet will come to them with a rather different understanding. So there is the vision recorded in prose in the book of Jeremiah:

> But this is the covenant that I will make with the house of Israel
> after those days, says the LORD: I will put my law within them,
> and I will write it on their hearts; and I will be their God, and
> they shall be my people. No longer shall they teach one another,
> or say to each other, "Know the LORD," for they shall all know
> me, from the least of them to the greatest, says the LORD; for I
> will forgive their iniquity, and remember their sin no more. (Jer
> 31:33–34)

This is to be something of a new covenant relationship, it no longer being written on tablets of stone, or even on scrolls, but will now be set within
people, on their hearts, within their inner being, surely intended to become
something truly of their inner lives. With the prophet Ezekiel we have not
dissimilar thoughts, the conveying of divine promises about the future, this
being about the fact that each generation is to be free of the sins of the past
generations, and so enabled to make a new start in life. Thus Ezekiel says,

> What do you mean by repeating this proverb concerning the
> land of Israel, "The parents have eaten sour grapes, and the chil-
> dren's teeth are set on edge"? As I live, says the LORD God, this
> proverb shall no more be used by you in Israel . . . . The person
> who sins shall die. A child shall not suffer for the iniquity of a
> parent, nor a parent suffer for the iniquity of a child; the righ-
> teousness of the righteous shall be his own, and the wickedness
> of the wicked shall be his own. (Ezek 18:2–3, 20)

Ezekiel proclaims that each generation has the opportunity to make a
new start. In the particular historical setting of the Jewish exile in Babylon,
it was through the sins of the "parents," that is an earlier generation, that
brought about the exile. But now, later, a new generation is not to be denied
the opportunity to begin again in life because of the sins of past generations.
No longer are these able to put the blame for present problems on past sins.
Here a new generation is promised a new start. That is, this new beginning
which politically speaking is due to certain human decisions to allow exiles
to return to their own lands, does also have theological aspects, in particular
that no longer can the present generation blame the peoples of the past and
their sins for present problems. Thus does the Old Testament speak here
of changing and developing ideas about the covenant relationship between
God and his people.

But we need to return to that scene of the people of Israel being in the
desert at the foot of the mountain called Horeb. For in what is portrayed
as that decidedly lengthy stop (Exod 19:1—40:38) not only were they told
about matters concerning the Israelite people's covenant relationship with

the Lord—and with each other—but they were moreover called to be very much involved in matters of worship. And clearly, what came at a much later time to be built in Jerusalem as a great temple for the worship of God, is here portrayed as being given by the Lord ("on the mountain") to his people as their holy place of worship.

As we observed earlier there is indeed much in the Old Testament on the subject of worship, a large proportion of the various books speaking one way or another about the worship of God, offered in various places, indeed varied worship, varied by its different emphases and aspects. Above all, the Old Testament speaks about the greatness, the majesty, and the holiness of the Lord. Thus is surely required of his people both the singing of his praises, and also the seeking his forgiveness of their sins. For a wide range of various aspects of worship—both of which were used in ancient times and which equally are still available for our use today—we have a large collection in a book with a whole variety of psalms; we have a good number of examples of people who give thanks for mercies received, and also a goodly number of examples of people praying about this situation or that, but throughout the whole is the glory and the awesomeness of the Lord God.

What, however, is perhaps something of a problem, a stumbling block, for many people in the contemporary Christian church in some parts of the world is the frequent talk of sacrifices and offerings, at times with fulsome details about how this and that sacrifice shall be prepared, and how it shall be offered. Yet the essential point is that the whole issue of sacrifices is related to that most serious matter of the sinfulness of the people, and that here is the way as they saw it for the securing of forgiveness of certain sins. Surely, here in these Old Testament details of the sacrificial system, with its talk of the seriousness of human sinfulness and the associated need to secure divine forgiveness and the opportunity to make a new start in life, is the source of Christian thanksgiving and praise for the new way of forgiveness they believe was both enabled, and brought about, through Christ Jesus. Nevertheless the Old Testament does also speak about other means for securing the forgiveness of sins, through other sacral acts, such as the Day of Atonement, or by seeking forgiveness of sins through prayers of confession to the Lord.

The Old Testament has a good deal to say about places of worship, both those that were authorized for such, and also those that were unacceptable. Thus we have talk of simple places of worship, likely in origin to have been places where a revelation or a mercy had been received or experienced, a tent or a tabernacle for such places as a desert setting, a temple in a settled and established place. These places were intended to be the sacred settings where sacrifices or other offerings were to be made, where prayer could to be made, where praises were to be offered. Yet further, such holy places—as in a particular way, the Jerusalem temple—were to be places to which pilgrimage might be made, as perhaps for which such a psalm as Ps 122, and even possibly that whole group of psalms bearing the title "A Song of Ascents" (Pss 120–34), was intended to be used, prayed, sung. There in that temple was a meeting place for God and his people, a place that through its very presence, and also through its various artefacts was what has been called a "non-verbal sign," an eloquent witness to the things, many of them inevitably invisible, of the Lord God. Nor to be forgotten in this regard were those who were responsible for the services, prayers and sacrifices, the actual care and presumably maintenance of the place of worship, not forgetting about those forbidden places of worship. Further, there was a real ministry and service involved in the teaching about these and other matters, namely those fulfilled by the priests and the Levites.

Finally, about worship it has to be said that one of the supreme treasures that has been passed onto us through the Old Testament is the whole collection of psalms, hallowed, as it were, through centuries of worship both in the Jewish and also in the Christian traditions. Here are indeed profound expressions of so many aspects of the worship of God, after so many centuries, still being used, such as, for example:

> I will bless the LORD at all times;
> his praise shall continually be in my mouth.
> My soul makes its boast in the LORD;
> let the humble hear and be glad.
> O magnify the LORD with me,
> and let us exalt his name together. (Ps 34:1–3)

> Have mercy on me, O God,
> according to your steadfast love;
> according to your abundant mercy
> blot out my transgressions.
> Wash me thoroughly from my iniquity,
> and cleanse me from my sin. (Ps 51:1–2)

Let us now return to that imaginary horizontal time-line, that historical time-line we thought about earlier, and thereby to one or two further aspects of our study. The Israelite community is generally described in the Old Testament as indeed a community, and at that a most special community. It is spoken of as being the special possession, the special people of the Lord, "For you are a people holy to the LORD your God; the LORD your God has chosen you out of all the peoples on earth to be his people, his treasured possession." (Deut 7:6) Is this perhaps what today we mean by the calling to be a "spiritual" people? One commentator has expressed it thus: "As 'holy' people, Israel is specially related to Yahweh in the same sense as a holy object or offering would be. That which is holy has an unmediated relationship to Yahweh." We are reminded of that relationship between the Lord's first created man, as this is described in the book of Genesis,

> "Then the LORD God formed man from the dust of the ground, and breathed into his nostrils the breath of life; and the man became a living being." (Gen 2:7)

And these people and all their descendants are for the Old Testament "holy" people, that is "different" people, those held in God's covenant love, called to be ever-close to God; forbidden to have idols, but rather to be recipients of Ten Commandments and also, through the years and through the centuries recipients of so many other laws and directions. They are a people who are given human leaders, not only priests and Levites, but also prophets, and kings—and ever for the Old Testament the search for the right and just and devoted king is made! Nor to be forgotten are all the people, those who are called to be God's people, the worshippers of God, the workers of God, and ever to have a care for the poor, the dispossessed, the refugees, the hungry.

Yet, in spite of all these being God's people, God's own possession, they are in the Old Testament portrayed as experiencing—both individually and corporately—those so-familiar setbacks in life, some being much greater and tragic than others. Thus in the Old Testament we read of no small number of people who cry out to God, some in anger, more in agony, others seeking help, others seeking some adequate explanations. The most extensive such writing by far, as we have seen, is the book of Job, yet the theme and the deep questions concerning how it is, and why it is, that those who are apparently living good and God-fearing lives do have suffering are to be found in other parts of the Old Testament, in psalms, in the books of Kings, in the so-called Wisdom Literature, and elsewhere. How valuable is this aspect of the Old Testament for our ongoing pursuit in the world both of the spiritual life, and also for meaning of such spiritual matters for other peoples. For indeed there is to be found in the Old Testament a truly honest view, and also a real overview of life; life indeed with many good things, and life also with some of these somewhat inexplicable happenings. As one scholar expressed it, "In broad terms, the Old Testament testifies to two contrasting aspects of spirituality; hope and confidence on the one hand, crisis and conflict on the other."

Yet further, it may be said that throughout the Old Testament we do truly have a worldly backdrop to what is being spoken about, and further a background which changes, sometimes for good, sometimes for ill. Indeed, what is said and done, taught and celebrated, is usually against that earthly backdrop. Thus, as we might say, when we are reading the Old Testament our feet are usually being kept very much "on the ground," that is, as we seek to live out, for example, those closing words of ch 28 of the book of Job,

> And he [the LORD] said to humankind,
> "Truly, the fear of the LORD, that is wisdom;
> and to depart from evil is understanding." (Job 28:28)

How is one to attempt some sort of summary of what we have been doing in this little work? How are we to organize all this varied material? One can hardly feel other than apparently Herman Melville did as he began chapter 82 of his work *Moby-Dick*, "The Honor and Glory of Whaling" when he said, "There are some enterprises in which a careful disorderliness is the true method." For while it is clear that the Old Testament has not been written so that it is able to speak to us in a direct and orderly way about matters of spirituality, yet within its pages there is a vast source of experience, and theological thought, that comes in so many different forms and styles, that reflects so many backgrounds and experiences, and that somewhat amazingly has come to be passed down through the ages and so has come to us, and does in fact—so I have argued in this work—speak to us about our spirituality today. Indeed, we should no doubt be reminded of that word of the Catholic Dogmatic Constitution on Divine Revelation (*Dei Verbum* 6.21), namely that "Scripture is the pure and perennial source of the spiritual life."

Thus we may yet be further emboldened to continue our search in the Old Testament for what possible help there is for our further and continuing guidance towards a spirituality for our lives in the world of today and tomorrow.

We consider briefly once again those four aspects of the matter we looked at earlier. For there surely is a sense of the sheer *length* of the Old Testament account: it covers years, and reigns, and even eras, giving us a whole series of historical scenarios where this people's spirituality is to be observed as it was being lived out. Here is recorded something of the religious experiences of a people in ever-changing earthly situations. Then there is the *depth* in the Old Testament documents, its writings, its records: that is, there is a probing down into humanity's ways, the good ways of life, the less-good ways, the evil possibilities, the physical necessities, and above all in those varied settings and contexts, the spiritual aspects of the constant seeking of the presence and guidance of the Lord for life in the world. There is also a *breadth* about these matters in the Hebrew Bible: for there are "others" referred to, other peoples, other nations, and perhaps before we come to the end of the Old Testament era these other peoples are coming to be taken more seriously, and the whole issue of living under empires is becoming more seriously grappled with. Moreover there are *heights* in these documents: some great spiritual ones. In fact, it could be said that the people of Israel and their leaders in their better moments are portrayed here as rising above their day-to-day problems and becoming engaged in considering the spiritual aspects of their lives. Perhaps it was through the ministries of their God-sent prophets, psalmists, wisdom writers, and others gifted with spiritual insights, that such engagement was being presented for the peoples and their national leaders to consider.

Essentially, it might be said that the Old Testament does in fact record and present vital aspects of the spiritual lives, and the spirituality, of a people whose calling was to live out such a life in the world, confronted as they were so constantly with earthly necessities and worldly problems. Maybe at times in the Old Testament records a certain earthiness may appear to be dominant, even almost overwhelming, but yet that surely should not make us lose sight of what at least some were determined to cling onto, namely the spiritual aspects in the many changes and chances of this mortal life. Further, in spite of any shortcomings in the lives of those spoken about in the Old Testament, there is no shortage of references to worship and the search in life for the Lord God—even though prophet and priest may condemn certain ways of worship, and most definitely certain of the chosen earthly settings for their acts of worship.

It could perhaps be that some of the foundational words about the Christian spiritual life were written many centuries ago, and mercifully preserved at the very beginning of what is the Hebrew and the Christian Bible:

> Then God said, "Let us make humankind in our image, according to our likeness . . ." (Gen 1:26a)

And then, as a final example from among so many possibilities we have considered in the foregoing little studies, we may hear a psalmist expressing what some of us might wish to call the reality of a life of Christian spirituality:

> You show me the path of life.
> In your presence there is fullness of joy;
> in your right hand are pleasures forevermore. (Ps 16:11)

Further Reading

INTRODUCTION

For current understandings of "spirituality" see the article "Spirituality" by the editor, Gordon S. Wakefield, *A Dictionary of Christian Spirituality*. London: SCM, 1983, 361–63, and from more recent times the essay by Sandra M. Schneiders, "Christian Spirituality; Definition, Methods and Types." In *The New Dictionary of Christian Spirituality*, edited by Philip Sheldrake, 1–6. London: SCM, 2005. See further, Philip Sheldrake, *Spirituality and Theology: Christian Living and the Doctrine of God*. London: Darton, Longman and Todd, 1998, in particular 33–64. On the Old Testament and Christian Spirituality see Christo Lombaard, *The Old Testament and Christian Spirituality: Theoretical and Practical Essays from a South African Perspective*. International Voices in Biblical Studies 2. Atlanta: Society of Biblical Literature, 2012, esp. 1–26, "The Old Testament and Christian Spirituality: Perspectives on the Undervaluation of the Old Testament in Christian Spirituality." I have found Alister E. McGrath, *Christian Spirituality: An Introduction*. Oxford: Blackwell, 1999, to be a helpful introduction to the general subject of spirituality, and my quotation on p.3 above is from p.2 of McGrath's work. See also R. W. L. Moberly, *The Bible in a Disenchanted Age: The Enduring Possibility of Christian Faith*. Grand Rapids: Baker Academic, 2018. Further works that may be found useful are Paula Gooder, *Body: Biblical Spirituality for the Whole Person*. London: SPCK, 2016; Angela Lou Harvey, *Spiritual Reading: A Study of the Christian Practice of Reading Scripture*. Cambridge: James Clarke, 2015. J. Gordon McConville, *Being Human in God's World: An Old Testament Theology of Humanity*. Grand Rapids: Baker Academic, 2016.

For the words of Thomas Merton on p.3 above see Rowan Williams, *A Silent Action: Engagements with Thomas Merton*. London: SPCK, 2013, 45.

The quotations on p.3 from Colin Alves and Mollie Batten are to be found in Eric James, ed., *Spirituality for Today*. London: SCM, 1968, 148 and 61 respectively. The citation from Rowan Williams on p.3 is from his *Being Disciples: Essentials of the Christian Life*. London: SPCK, 2016, 75–76. The quotation from Saint Augustine on p.5, is from his *Confessions*. Translated by R. S. Pine-Coffin. Harmondsworth: Penguin, 1961, 21.

The quotation on p.6 concerning "heart" is from Walter Eichrodt, *Theology of the Old Testament*. Vol. 2. Translated by J. A. Baker. London: SCM, 1967, 143. The quotation on p.15 is from *Revelations of Divine Love* and comes from "The Long Text," chapter 78. See Julian of Norwich, *Revelations of Divine Love*. Translated by Elizabeth Spearing. London: Penguin, 1998, 169.

1: LIFE IN CREATION AND COVENANT

For concise and user-friendly commentaries on the books of Genesis and Exodus I suggest: Clare Amos, *The Book of Genesis*. Epworth Commentaries. Peterborough: Epworth, 2004; Richard Coggins, *The Book of Exodus*. Epworth Commentaries. Peterborough: Epworth, 2000. The commentator referred to on p.20 is Claus Westermann, *Genesis 1–11: A Commentary*. Translated by John J. Scullion. London: SPCK, 1984, 158. The reference on p.26 is to John I. Durham, *Exodus*. Word Biblical Commentary 3. Waco: Word, 1987, 262. For the series of prayers mentioned on p.30, see my *Greatly To Be Praised: The Old Testament and Worship*. Eugene, OR: Pickwick, 2016, 192–94. The reference on p.32 is to *The Cloud of Unknowing*. Translated by Clifton Wolters. London: Penguin, 1961, 91–92. On the Ten Commandments, p.33, see Carl E. Braaten and Christopher R. Seitz, *I Am the Lord Your God: Christian Reflections on the Ten Commandments*. Cambridge: Eerdmans, 2005; David L. Baker, *The Decalogue: Living as the People of God*. Downers Grove, IL: InterVarsity, 2017. For the subject of worship in the Old Testament, see above for my, *Greatly To Be Praised*. For the reference to Luther on p.33 see Robert Louis Wilken, "Keeping the Commandments." In *I Am the Lord Your God: Christian Reflections on the Ten Commandments*, edited by Carl E. Braaten and Christopher Seitz, 23–52. Grand Rapids: Eerdmans, 2005. The quotation on p.34 from Julian of Norwich is taken from *Revelations of Divine Love* (Short Text and Long Text), Julian of Norwich. Translated by Elizabeth Spearing. London: Penguin, 1998, 7. For the quotation from Augustine on p.34 see Saint Augustine, *Confessions*. Translated by R. S. Pine-Coffin. London: Penguin, 1961, 21.

2: LIFE WITH DELIVERANCE AND JUDGEMENT

For the twin themes of deliverance and judgement in the Old Testament see Walter Brueggemann, *Theology of the Old Testament: Testimony, Dispute, Advocacy*. Minneapolis: Fortress, 1997, 173–81 and 373–85. For the lament themes in the biblical Psalms see William P. Brown, *Psalms*. Interpreting Biblical Texts. Nashville: Abingdon, 2010, esp. 138–44; S. E. Gillingham, *The Poems and Psalms of the Hebrew Bible*. Oxford Bible Series. Oxford: OUP, 1994, esp. 149–56, 214–19, 244–45, 271; Simon P. Stocks, *Songs for Suffering: Praying the Psalms in Times of Trouble*. Peabody, MA: Hendrickson, 2017. On the Psalms, see also, John Eaton, *The Psalms, A Historical and Spiritual Commentary with Introduction and New Translation*. London: Continuum, 2005; John Eaton, *Psalms for Life: Hearing and Praying the Book of Psalms*. London: SPCK, 2006; Adrian Curtis, *Psalms*. Epworth Commentaries. Peterborough: Epworth, 2004.

As far as biblical concordances are concerned, the two classic ones, based on words used in the King James Version of the Bible, are those respectively of Alexander Cruden and of Robert Young. More recent ones are: *New Revised Standard Version Exhaustive Concordance*, edited by Bruce Metzger; *The New Revised Standard Version Concordance* (including Apocrypha and Deuterocanonical books) edited by John Kohlenberger III; *The Concise Concordance to the New Revised Standard Version*, edited by John R. Kohlenberger III. Further, *The New Oxford Annotated Bible* (New Revised Standard Version) has a concordance.

The quotation on p.43 is from R. W. L. Moberly, *Old Testament Theology: Reading the Hebrew Bible as Christian Scripture*. Grand Rapids: Baker Academic, 2013, 56. See further for Moberly's treatment of the problem of Deut 7:1–3 in the above work, 58–62. The quotation on p.50 is from Thomas à Kempis, *The Imitation of Christ*. Translated by E. M. Blaiklock. London: Hodder and Stoughton, 1979, 78.

3: LIFE OF WORSHIP

On the subject of this chapter see my *Greatly To Be Praised: The Old Testament and Worship*. Eugene, OR: Pickwick, 2016; Walter Brueggemann, *Worship in Ancient Israel: An Essential Guide*. Nashville: Abingdon, 2005. The references regarding anthropological investigations on p.54 are to E. E. Evans-Pritchard, *Nuer Religion*. Oxford: Clarendon, 1956; and to Mary Douglas in her work, *Purity and Danger: An Analysis of Concepts of Pollution and Taboo*. Harmondsworth: Penguin, 1970. On p.55 for the references about issues of forgiveness of sins being spoken about in the New Testament see, K. Grayston, *Dying, We Live: A New Enquiry into the Death of Christ in the New Testament*. London: Darton, Longman and Todd, 1990, 338–75; Morna D. Hooker, *Not Ashamed of the Gospel: New Testament Interpretations of the Death of Christ*. Carlisle: Paternoster, 1994, 112–30. For the reference on p.57 to "types" of the biblical psalms see, for example, John Day, *Psalms*. Old Testament Guides. Sheffield: JSOT, 1990. For the reference on pp.59–60 to the human experience of suffering spoken about in Pss 37, 49, and 73, see my *Where is the God of Justice? The Old Testament and Suffering*. Eugene, OR: Pickwick, 2011, 58–61, 81–84, 100–104. The work by Susan Gillingham referred to on p.66 is the very full and helpful volume, *Psalms Through the Centuries: Volume One*. Blackwell Bible Commentaries. Oxford: Blackwell, 2008. See in particular the various sections about liturgy and psalmody, 40–46, 68–71, 120–23, 131–63, 228–30, 254–66. For the closing reference to Gen 28:16–17, p.68, see the remarks of Clare Amos, *Genesis*. Epworth Commentaries. Peterborough: Epworth, 2004, 180–83. For the quotation from the sermon of John of Damascus, p.68 see Eugen J. Pentiuc, *The Old Testament in the Eastern Orthodox Tradition*. Oxford: Oxford University Press, 2014, 235.

4: LIFE IN COMMUNITY

The quotation on p.72 is from Brevard S. Childs, *Exodus: A Commentary*. Old Testament Library. London: SCM, 1974, 367. The reference on p.72 is to Walter Brueggemann, *Theology of the Old Testament: Testimony, Dispute, Advocacy*. Minneapolis: Fortress, 1997, 417; while the comment concerning Num 23:9 on p.72 is by Eryl W. Davies, *Numbers*. New Century Bible Commentary. London: Marshall Pickering, 1995, 257. For the blood in sacrifices spoken about on p.75 see ch. 3 above "Life of Worship," p.54. On "atonement" see ch. 3 above, pp.54–55 and also my *Greatly To Be Praised*, 165, 166, 170–75. For the Old Testament and ethics see ch. 7 below, "Life with Ethical Concerns." On the word "atonement" on 75 see ch. 3 above pp.54–55 For the reference to Priests and Levites on p.75 see my *Greatly To Be Praised*, 71–88. On priests, Levites, kings, prophets and sages on pp. 75-82 see Joseph Blenkinsopp, *Sage, Priest, Prophet: Religious and Intellectual Leadership in Ancient Israel*. Louisville: Westminster John Knox, 1995. For the reference on p.75 to Levites explaining the message of the reading of the Law, see ch. 3 above, pp.63–64. On spiritual leadership see also the article Mark S. Aidoo, "Empowering Followers in the Politics of Spiritual Leadership: A Narrative Critical study of 1 Samuel 1:1–28." *Expository Times* 128/8 (May

2017) 365–75. H. G. M. Williamson, *He Has Shown You What Is Good: Old Testament Justice Then and Now.* The Trinity Lectures, Singapore, 2011. Cambridge: Lutterworth, 2012. For the reference to Calvin and his lectures in Geneva, pp.83-84, see John Calvin, *Jonah, Micah, and Nahum.* Translated by John Owen. The Geneva Series of Commentaries. Edinburgh: Banner of Truth Trust, 1986, 343. For the quotation from Thomas Merton, p.84, see his *The Seven Storey Mountain.* New York: Harcourt, Brace, 1948, 169.

5: LIFE IN A CHANGING WORLD

The quotation on p.93 is from W. Brueggemann, *The Land.* Overtures to Biblical Theology. London: SPCK, 1978, 45. For the reference to states and borders on p.100, see the Book of Ruth chs 2–4; see further, Peter H. W. Lau and Gregory Goswell, *Unceasing Kindness: A Biblical Theology of Ruth.* London: Apollos, 2016. For the reference on p.101 see, *The Cloud of Unknowing.* Translated by Clifton Wolters. Harmondsworth: Penguin, 1961, 90.

6: LIFE WITH QUESTIONS

On this whole subject see Michael E. W. Thompson, *Where Is the God of Justice? The Old Testament and Suffering.* Eugene, OR: Pickwick, 2011. James L. Crenshaw has written extensively on the subject of the Old Testament and questions about sufferings, one of his contributions being *Defending God: Biblical Responses to the Problem of Evil.* Oxford: Oxford University Press, 2005. See also Robert Davidson, *The Courage to Doubt: Exploring an Old Testament Theme.* London: SCM, 1983, and further, Simon P. Stocks, *Songs for Suffering: Praying the Psalms in Times of Trouble.* Peabody, MA: Hendrickson, 2017. For the reference on p.114 to the content of a certain letter of John Keats, see John Keats, *The Letters of John Keats,* edited by M. B. Forman, 3rd ed. London: Oxford University Press, 1947. For the reference on pp.117-118 to the so-called Servant Songs in Isa 40–55 see my commentary *Isaiah 40–66.* Epworth Commentaries. Peterborough: Epworth, 2001; xxiii–xxiv, 100–114; now also republished as *Isaiah 40–66,* Eugene, OR: Wipf & Stock, 2012, xxiii–xxiv, 100–114. The book by Robert Gordis quoted on p.119 is his *The Book of God and Man: A Study of Job.* Chicago: University of Chicago Press, 1965, 134. For the reference to the two contrasting aspects of spirituality in the Old Testament on p.119 see, J. L. Houlden's article "Bible, Spirituality of the." In *A Dictionary of Christian Spirituality,* edited by Gordon S. Wakefield, 48–51. London: SCM, 1983. See especially 49. For the quotation from *Revelations of Divine Love* on p.120, see Julian of Norwich, *Revelations of Divine Love*. Translated by Elizabeth Spearing. London: Penguin, 1998, 24.

7: LIFE WITH ETHICAL CONCERNS

For a recent work that faces up to the series of problems there are in the Old Testament over issues concerning ethics, and that also suggests some ways forward, we can hardly do better than go to Eryl W. Davies, *The Immoral Bible: Approaches to Biblical Ethics*. London: T. & T. Clark, 2010. See also John Dominic Crossan, *Jesus and the Violence of Scripture: How to Read the Bible and Still Be a Christian*. London: SPCK, 2015. For articles on Old Testament ethics see the following: James Muilenburg, "Old Testament Ethics." in *Dictionary of Christian Ethics*, edited by John Macquarrie, 235–27. London: SCM, 1974; Henry McKeating, "Old Testament Ethics." In *A New Dictionary of Christian Ethics*, edited by James F. Childress and John Macquarrie, 433–37. London: SCM, 1986; William C. Spohn, "Ethics and Spirituality." In *The New Dictionary of Christian Spirituality*, edited by Philip Sheldrake, 284–86. London: SCM, 2005. For a full work on this subject see Bruce C. Birch, *Let Justice Roll Down: The Old Testament, Ethics, and Christian Life*. Louisville: Westminster/John Knox, 1991; Cyril S. Rodd, *Glimpses of a Strange Land: Studies in Old Testament Ethics*. Edinburgh: T. & T. Clark, 2001; John Barton, *Understanding Old Testament Ethics; Approaches and Explorations*. Louisville: Westminster John Knox, 2003; *The Bible in Ethics: The Second Sheffield Colloquium*, edited by John Rogerson, Margaret Davies, M. Daniel Carroll R. Sheffield, UK: Sheffield Academic Press, 1995. See also, Richard S. Briggs, *Fairer Sex: Spiritual Readings of Four Old Testament Passages about Men and Women*. Grove Biblical Series 77. Cambridge: Grove Books, 2015. The work spoken of on p.135 is Thomas à Kempis, *The Imitation of Christ*. Translated by E. M. Blaiklock. London: Hodder and Stoughton, 1990, and the words quoted are to be found in this edition on p. 27.

8: LIFE WITH A FUTURE

The quotation on p.140 is from E.W. Heaton, *Daniel*. Torch Bible Commentary. London: SCM, 1956, 247. See also N. W. Porteous, *Daniel*. Old Testament Library. London: SCM, 1965, 171. The quotation on p.148 is from K. Baltzer, *Deutero-Isaiah: A Commentary on Isaiah 40–55*. Translated by Margaret Kohl. Hermeneia Commentary. Minneapolis: Fortress, 2001, 311. For the quotation from a sermon of John Donne on p.150 see John Moses,

One Equall Light: An Anthology of the Writings of John Donne. Norwich: Canterbury, 2003, 316. See also the work, Philip S. Johnson, *Shades of Sheol: Death and Afterlife in the Old Testament.* Downers Grove, IL: Apollos, 2002.

9: THE OLD TESTAMENT AND CHRISTIAN SPIRITUALITY: CONCLUSIONS

The quotation on p.154 from John Calvin, *Genesis.* Translated by John King. London: Banner of Truth Trust, 1965, 57. The reference on p.160 is to R. D. Nelson, *Deuteronomy.* Old Testament Library. Louisville and London: Westminster John Knox, 2004, 100. For the J. L. Houlden reference, on p.160, see his article, "Bible, Spirituality of the." In *A Dictionary of Christian Spirituality*, edited by Gordon S. Wakefield, 48–51. London: SCM, 49. For the reference to Moby-Dick on p.161, see Herman Melville, *Moby-Dick.* Harmondsworth: Penguin, 1986, 469. The reference on p.161 to the Catholic Dogmatic Constitution on Divine Revelation (*Dei Verbum* 6.21), is from the article by Sandra Schneiders, "Spirituality and Scripture." In *The New Dictionary of Christian Spirituality*, edited by Philip Sheldrake, 62–67. London: SCM, 2005, 63.

Index of Subjects

Index of Biblical References

Lightning Source UK Ltd.
Milton Keynes UK
UKHW020148060121
376487UK00005B/201

9 781532 673108